The Changing Status of Women

Olivia Bennett

Bell & Hyman

Acknowledgements

The author and publishers would like to thank the following for permission to reproduce photographs, illustrations or extracts from books, newspapers and magazines. (Extracts have also been acknowledged in the text.)

Photographs and illustrations
Associated Press Ltd   43(L)
Barnaby's Picture Library   41
BBC Hulton Picture Library   6(B), 10(T&B), 12(B), 15(B), 16(T), 19, 20, 21(T), 22(B), 24, 29, 30(T&C), 32(B), 36(B), 37
Format (Judy Harrison) 4, (Joanne O'Brien) 39, (Michael Ann Mullen) 40(B), (Maggie Murray) 43(R)
Sally and Richard Greenhill   5, 44, 46
Imperial War Museum   23, 34(T)
Low Pay Unit (GLC)   40(T)
The Mansell Collection   6(T), 9, 13, 14, 15(T), 22(T), 25, 27, 28, 30(B), 34(B), 35, 36(T), 38(L)
Mary Evans Picture Library   7, 16(B), 18, 21(B), 26
The Marie Stopes Clinic, London 32(T)
The Metropolitan Museum of Art, New York: (The Elisha Whittesley Collection, The Elisha Whittesley Fund, 1959   (59.533.324) 11
Press Association   45(T)
Punch   12(T)
Royal Shakespeare Company   8
Virago   45(B)

Extracts
All book references are positioned below the extract, or extracts, to which they refer.
Northanger Abbey, Jane Austen, Chatto & Windus   4
Not in God's Image; Women in History, Ed. Martines & O'Faolain (3 extracts) 7, (Rousseau) 10
The Weaker Vessel, Antonia Fraser, Methuen   8, 9 (3 extracts)
Holiday House, Hardcastle, Longman   12
A Woman's Place, Elizabeth Roberts, Basil Blackwell   13
Suffragettes and Votes for Women, L. E. Snellgrove, Longman   23 (2 extracts) 34
Ordinary Lives, Carol Adams, Virago   14 (1 extract), 20
Fenwomen, Mary Chamberlain, History Workshop Series, Routledge and Kegan Paul   14 (2 extracts), 15 (3 extracts), 24, 46 (2 extracts)
Appeal of One Half of the Human Race, Women, Against the Pretensions of the Other Half, Men. William Thompson, Virago   19
Strong-minded Women and Other Lost Voices from Nineteenth Century England, Ed. Janet Horowitz Murray, Penguin   17, 24 (and caption 24) 26
Dutiful Daughters, McCrindle and Rowbotham, Allen Lane   25
Women, Winifred Holtby   28
There's Always Been a Women's Movement This Century, Dale Spender, Pandora   31 (Constance Rover extract), 32 (Hallinan extract), 39 (Hallinan extract)
Women: A World Report, Ed. Debbie Taylor, Methuen   33, 43
What did you do in the War, Mum?, Age Exchange Publications   36 (3 extracts), 37 (6 extracts), 38

Girls are Powerful, Ed. Hemmings, Sheba Feminist Publishers   15, 40, 44 (2 extracts), 46
Kitchen Sink, or Swim? Women in the Eighties – the choices, Deidre Sanders with Jane Reed, Pelican 40 (2 extracts), 41 (3 extracts)
Polly Toynbee, *The Guardian*, 9.2.87.,   41
The Role of Women, Sharon Gould, Macdonald Educational   31, 42, 46
Jill Tweedie, *The Guardian*, 28.12.79.
Equal Opportunities Commission (from DES statistics)   75/6

Further Reading

Many of the books mentioned in the acknowledgements have useful bibliographies. Some particularly fruitful sources of background material on women's lives are:

Women in history series, Cambridge Educational
Ordinary Lives by Carol Adams, Virago
Fenwomen, History Workshop series, Routledge and Kegan Paul
What did you do in the War, Mum? Age Exchange Publications
The Weaker Vessel by Antonia Fraser, Methuen
Dutiful Daughters by McCrindle and Rowbotham, Allen Lane
The Motherland by Elyse Dodgson, Heinemann Educational
In Her Own Time series, Hamish Hamilton

Published in 1987 by
BELL & HYMAN
An imprint of Unwin Hyman Limited
Denmark House
37–39 Queen Elizabeth Street
London SE1 2QB

British Library Cataloguing in Publication Data
Bennett, Olivia
   The changing status of women.——(Knowing British history topics).
   1. Women——Social conditions
   I. Title   II. Series
   305.4'2'09   HW1121

ISBN 0 7135 2623 8

Typeset in Great Britain by
Latimer Trend & Company Ltd, Plymouth

Printed and bound by
Bell & Bain Ltd., Glasgow

Contents

Words printed in italics are explained in the Glossary

To the teacher

This book is about changes in the political, economic, social, legal and occupational status of women in Britain. It explores how these were brought about by a combination of historical circumstances, the activities of individual women who influenced ideas and attitudes, and the determined collective efforts of masses of ordinary women.

The book's approach is particularly useful for those pupils working towards GCSE examinations as it combines evidence-based activities with the acquisition of historical skills in a topic of increasing importance in GCSE syllabuses. There are many short extracts from contemporary speeches, writings and interviews. Questions cater for mixed ability classes and relate to the historical facts, the source material and the illustrations. There are a number of suggestions for oral and discussion work, as well as written, visual and statistical work. Project work in oral history is also included. Pupils could research and write short biographies on some of the individuals mentioned in the text.

There is a glossary of words italicised in the narrative and the quoted extracts but it would be advisable to make sure that pupils understand certain key words and concepts before embarking on the text, notably 'emancipation', 'suffrage', 'expectations', 'status' and 'patriarchy'.

The text explores legislative and other changes from the Middle Ages to the present day. As the early chapters make clear, the labour-intensive nature of domestic responsibilities and poor educational opportunities have meant that, until recent years, documentary material by women on their lives is relatively scarce. It is particularly hard to find material on ordinary working women before the nineteenth century, and on immigrant women generally. This means that a survey like this inevitably contains more information about middle class women, but care should be taken to stress that a lack of recorded history does not imply a lack of contribution to society.

There are many books, some autobiographical, which contain interesting background on women's lives and experiences (see Further Reading opposite). Local women's studies and history groups may also be able to provide information. *Discovering Women's History* by Deidre Beddoe, Pandora Press, is full of helpful suggestions and advice on sources. The position of women today is touched upon in the final chapters. There is plenty of social studies material which should be used to expand this exploration of the current movements and issues.

Chapter 1 Hardly Any Women At All?

This book is about the changes in women's *status* in Britain. 'Status' means a person's standing or position in society. The sort of things which define a person's status in society are:

1) laws – how do they treat a person?
2) education – what are people taught?
3) employment – what are the jobs that people can or cannot do?
4) expectations – what are people encouraged to do and to get out of life?
5) politics – can people vote or work in politics?
6) family life – what sort of role are people expected to play in the family?

   Words like 'encourage', 'expect' and 'treat' are important in this list. They appear to be quite harmless words – at least, they do not seem as fierce as 'order', 'demand', or 'forbid'. Yet the *expectations* of the society we live in can be almost as powerful as its laws. If we grow up thinking that we can only achieve certain things, because these are what people expect from us, it can make it almost impossible for us to attempt to do anything different – even if there is no actual law preventing us. So changes in status involve changing people's ideas as well as laws.

Women's history

Finding out about women's status means exploring women's history. Discovering the part women have played in the past is not always easy. This is how one of Jane Austen's heroines described her experience of history books:

> '... history, solemn history, I confess I cannot be interested in. The quarrels of popes and kings, with wars and pestilence on every page; the men so good-for-nothing, and hardly any women at all – it is very tiresome.'
>
> (Catherine Norland in *Northanger Abbey*)

Until recently, history as it was written and taught usually concentrated on the affairs of royalty and people of power – mostly men. It was about their actions in war, *diplomacy*, politics and trade. One of the few areas of women's history

Women's history was a neglected subject until quite recently. Today, many colleges run courses in Women's Studies. There are publishers and bookshops which deal only with books by and about women. Local history groups talk to elderly people in the community and record their experiences. It will be easier for future generations to learn about the part women play in society.

which was discussed was the *suffragettes*' fight for the vote at the turn of the nineteenth century. Historians often gave the impression that the vote was the only concern of women seeking *emancipation*. In fact it was not the only demand made, nor was it the first time this particular change had been sought. Women had long been seeking greater *equality* in what they could learn, what they could own, how the law treated them and what they could do with their lives. If you look at the Time Chart you'll see some of the changes which were achieved before the National Union of Women's *Suffrage* was even founded.

Finding out

One of the difficulties in uncovering women's history is that until the seventeenth century very little was written by women themselves about their ideas and experiences. Before this time those who could read and write were mostly men, and they were usually either men of wealth or in the Church. From the early 1600s, however, women of the upper classes began to receive some education. But it was not until the end of the nineteenth century that education became available to everyone, rich or poor. Thus, until less than a hundred years ago, any information we do have about ordinary women's lives is rarely written by themselves, from their own point of view.

So to find out about the lives of women in the centuries when most of them, through no fault of their own, were *illiterate*, we have to search through the few surviving letters and diaries written by upper class women, and comb through the writings of men for some references to women. Pictures can help us, too. Medieval paintings, for example, tell us quite a lot about the kind of work women did then. Other sources are official reports, household accounts, family wills, parish registers, and popular songs and stories. All these help to build up a picture of women's daily lives and their place in society at a particular time.

Much more of this kind of research has been done now. It shows us that, although the nineteenth century stands out as an age when many important changes in the status of women in Britain began to take place, they were the result of centuries of earlier thought, discussion and effort. The desire for greater equality was not new. Although it was often impossibly hard for most women to break out of the role which was expected of them, in every age there were some – such as Mary Astell, Aphra Behn and Mary Wollstonecraft – who dared to publicly express the

hope that there were wider possibilities for women. Every century had its women travellers, scholars and pioneers who did escape from their expected role in life. They can't have been alone in their *ambitions*. They had friends and supporters. There must have been many other women who dreamed of a different way of life and whose achievements – and failures – we know little or nothing of, because they were not recorded.

---

1. **Choose one or two history books you use regularly. Dividing the work among the class, find out how often they mention women and how this compares with the number of men mentioned. How often do women appear in the pictures? How often does the information about women present their point of view? Discuss the reasons for your findings.**

---

2. **The writer Virginia Woolf described the life of Britain's millions of housewives as 'this curious silent unrepresented life'. What do you think she meant by this?**

---

3. **Talk to your grandmother or a woman of similar age. Ask her to tell you about her life: her education, hobbies, work, family, home etc. Write down or record her memories. Compare her experiences with your own or those of your mother, sister or cousin. Describe the differences and similarities between them, taking care to think about expectations and ambitions as well as practical details.**

How much do you know about the life of your own grandmother or great-grandmother? Her education? Her ambitions? Did she have a job? If so, was this because she chose to or she had to? We often know much more about the lives of our forefathers – the job they did, perhaps the war they fought in – than about our foremothers, particularly if they were housewives.

Chapter 2 Pre-industrial Society

During the late eighteenth and early nineteenth century, Britain changed from being an agricultural society – in which the majority of people lived and worked in the countryside – to an industrial one. To find out how this important change affected women's status we need to explore 'pre-industrial' society.

The Middle Ages

During the Middle Ages, the large landowners were the most powerful people in the country. Marriages of the wealthy were often arranged in order to increase ownership of land. Details were usually decided by the fathers of the couple. The daughter of a landowner had little choice over whom she married, but once she became lady of the manor she sometimes had a lot of responsibility. Husbands were often away fighting or attending the king's court. Wives remained at home, in charge of large estates and all the people who lived and worked there.

The only women to own land in their own right were usually widows who had been left property by their husbands. In some towns special laws and customs gave married tradeswomen certain rights and independence. There were quite a lot of nuns, who were the only women to have the chance of an education. However, the vast majority of women – rich or poor – had no legal rights, owned nothing and were rarely educated.

Medieval women worked in the fields with men, sharing the agricultural work.

The bulk of the population were ordinary working people. Running a medieval home involved a heavy workload and many different skills. The family's food and clothes all had to be made from raw materials. Women did every kind of job, from hard labour in the fields and running shops and businesses in the towns to skilled craftwork, such as silk weaving. As the medieval period wore on, it became more difficult for women to enter skilled trades. They received lower wages than men for the same work. They were accused of adding to unemployment, and suffered restrictions like this:

'many people – likely men to do the King service in his wars and in the defence of this his land, and sufficiently learned in the said craft go *vagrant*

Many farming men and women added to the family income by spinning and weaving cloth. They worked together at home, the women usually doing the spinning.

and unoccupied ... therefore no person of the said craft of weavers [in Bristol] from this day forward, may set, put or hire, his said wife, daughter or maid to such occupation ... upon pain of [a fine].'

(Statement made in Bristol, 1461)

---

1. The writer is saying that men ought to have priority over women for employment. Why do you think he mentions that the men are likely to be brave soldiers?

Skilled women workers fought to keep their position. In 1455 the 'silk women' of London marched through the streets protesting against foreign goods being brought into the country and damaging their trade. However, by the end of the sixteenth century most women had been squeezed out of the skilled trades. Some became domestic servants in the homes of rich city dwellers. In the textile industry they became 'unskilled' button-holers and seamstresses.

Few medieval women had the education or opportunity to record their experiences, thoughts and feelings. One woman who has told us about the period is Christine de Pisan. She lived, in France, from 1363 to 1431. She was the first woman that we know of to earn her living by writing. One of the things which affected society's view of women was that the Church at this time often presented woman as an evil temptress. A famous Italian poet described woman as 'a real devil, an enemy of peace'. De Pisan tried to present a positive view of women, pointing out

The Church had a powerful influence in the Middle Ages. Many priests taught that women were deceitful and likely to tempt men to sin, just as Eve had tempted Adam in the Garden of Eden.

that they did not cause the wars and fighting which constantly ravaged medieval society. She also wrote:

'If it were customary to send little girls to school and to teach them the same subjects as are taught to boys, they would learn just as fully and would understand the *subtleties* of all arts and sciences. ... If they understand less it is because they do not go out and see so many different places and things but stay at home and mind their own work. For there is nothing which teaches a reasonable creature so much as the experience of many things.'

(*City of Ladies*)

---

2. What does Christine de Pisan believe would happen if girls had both more education and experience? Continue her argument in your own words.

The sixteenth century

Between 1500 and 1650, England's towns, especially London, began to grow in size and importance. However, the majority of the population still lived in the country. Women shared the agricultural work with men. In seasons when there was less farm work, families took on other jobs, especially in the textile industry. Cloth was usually spun and woven at home, with the family again sharing the work. Women were often involved in other trades, such as brewing beer and baking bread. They were partners with men in the family economy.

During the sixteenth century England was ruled by one of her greatest monarchs, Queen Elizabeth I (1558–1603). She was respected for her intelligence and her skill in politics and diplomacy. Yet in spite of this shining example, most people were in agreement that women were less intelligent than men. Once they married, any land or money they had became the property of their husbands. So rich women were valued for the wealth they brought to a family and poor women for the work they did within the family, but they were regarded as inferior. This is how a sixteenth century lawyer described women:

'Every [woman] is a sort of infant. ... It is seldom, almost never, that a married woman can have any action to use her *wit* only in her own name: her husband is ... her *prime mover*, without whom she cannot do much at home, and less *abroad* ...'

---

3. To whom are women compared above? What does this say about their status at the time?

7

Chapter 3 The Seventeenth Century

By the seventeenth century it had become more common for upper class women to learn to read and write. We begin to hear women's voices more clearly through letters, poems and diaries. Two particular women, Aphra Behn and Mary Astell, spoke out more loudly than most.

In 1694, Mary Astell had written *A Serious Proposal to the Ladies for the Advancement of their Time and Greatest Interest*. It was one of the first demands for higher education for women. Astell argued that men were not superior to women but that men had simply organised society so that women were unable to develop themselves as men's equals. She hated the way this *patriarchal* society made women dependent on men. She drew up plans for a women's college. Her ideas were ridiculed by many powerful men of her time. She had to put up with, as she put it, 'those wise Jests and Scoffs that are put upon a Woman of Sense and Learning, a *philosophical* Lady as she is called by way of Ridicule.' The college was never built (no such college opened until 1848).

1. People opposed to Astell's ideas refused to take them seriously. Do you think treating them as a joke was a more effective way of dismissing them than arguing against them? If so, why?

Petticoat-authors

Aphra Behn (1640–89) broke many of society's rules by becoming a successful writer. She too found her achievement ridiculed. She was called a

A scene from a 1986 production of The Rover. *It was written in 1677 by Aphra Behn, England's first successful woman playwright, poet and novelist.*

'petticoat-author'. Behn was unusually brave and adventurous. However, as she herself said, the reason she became the first English woman to support herself by writing was not because most other women lacked talent. It was because they were denied knowledge and a *classical* education. Upper class girls were not taught the Classics (Latin or Greek), as their brothers were. They learnt enough mathematics to do the household accounts, and skills such as needlework, singing and a little French conversation. This is how one woman described the way she was educated:

'As if we were for nothing else designed
But made, like puppets, to divert mankind.'
(Lady Chudleigh)

2. Explain in your own words this woman's complaint about her education.

3. Discuss the phrase 'petticoat-author'. Is it a compliment?

Behn's own ignorance of Latin meant she could not write in the classical style which became increasingly popular. Lack of Latin also limited women working in one of the few traditional female professions of the time: nursing. No nurse or midwife could hope to become a doctor because Latin was the language of medicine. Latin was the key to higher education and training; without it, women who wished to study were at a great disadvantage.

Elizabeth I had encouraged learning among the ladies at her court, but James I, who succeeded her, had a poor opinion of women's intelligence. He refused to allow his own daughter to learn Latin, saying 'To make women learned and foxes tame had the same effect; to make them more cunning.'

4. How did the lack of a classical education affect women?

5. What was James I's view of the effect of educating women?

During the Civil War, the 'weaker sex' demonstrated just how brave, resourceful and tough they could be. They played important roles in the fighting, and in the political arguments.

Civil War

A combination of character and circumstances encouraged Astell and Behn to explore their talents. But throughout these early centuries, the difficulty for most women was that circumstances rarely provided them with opportunities to prove their worth. The structure of society discouraged it. The lack of a proper means of birth control meant that most women spent many years bearing and rearing children. This not only consumed their time but also weakened their health.

War is one time when opportunities increase for women to demonstrate their abilities. Society is turned upside down and the old rules do not always apply. Above all, men cannot afford to ignore women's skills.

The Civil War which took place in England between 1642 and 1660 was no exception. It was a fierce battle for power between the supporters of the monarchy and those who wanted Cromwell and his 'roundheads' to rule the country. It was a time of great change and turmoil, in which women often played an active role. They helped to defend their homes and communities against attack, ran their estates and helped political refugees. Willingly or unwillingly, they had to take on 'men's' work – and they proved just how brave, clever and resourceful they could be. They also became much more involved in the discussion of political ideas. They learnt to hold their position in arguments with men. Some wrote petitions to Parliament asking for the release of political prisoners. From this time on, an increasing number of women writers had their work published.

6. Imagine it is the 1640s and you are writing a letter to a friend abroad. Describe how the Civil War has changed the lives of women.

Although men were grateful for women's courage during the Civil War, after it was over they were soon describing women as the 'weaker sex'. However, 'weakness' increasingly became a quality to be prized. Women were praised for being more 'delicate' and 'pure' than men – but that, of course, meant they needed a man to look after them and 'protect' them from the burden of such responsibilities as owning property.

7. Study these extracts from seventeenth century poems and letters. Describe the attitudes towards women which they reveal. (Perhaps these phrases will help you: 'best seen and not heard'; 'speak only when spoken to'; 'foolish but decorative'; 'no right to an opinion'.)

'Alas! a woman who attempts the pen,
Such an intruder on the rights of men.'

'remember thou art a Maid, and such ought thy modesty to bee, that thou shouldst scarce speak, but when thou answerest.'

'Love a Woman! you're an Ass
  'Tis a most *insipid* passion
To choose out for your Happiness
  The silliest part of God's Creation.'

Chapter 4   The Eighteenth Century

Mary Wollstonecraft (1759–97).

During the eighteenth century, England underwent major social and economic changes. Developments in machinery, energy sources, materials and methods of transport slowly changed the country's working life. By 1800, England was well on the way to becoming the world's first industrial nation.

Trades gradually became more specialised. People worked in small workshops rather than in the home. Machinery was invented which speeded up textile and agricultural production. New industries developed. Workshops grew into factories. More and more people left the rural areas and moved to the cities. As the home became separated from the workplace, working class women were forced out into factories. Single girls gained some independence but married women at home lost their chance to earn money. They were no longer the economic equals of their husbands, as they had been when they worked together as a family unit.

The idea of the 'family wage' developed. The theory was that men should be paid more because they worked to support a family and women only took jobs for 'pin-money' – to buy little extras. And women's work in the home, of course, was unpaid and so began not to count as 'real' work.

Middle class women were not meant to work at all. Their husbands went out into the world of business and politics while they stayed at home, increasingly cut off from anything outside the family and the household. Naturally their interests narrowed. By the time Mary Wollstonecraft was writing (in the 1790s), people generally regarded women as being incapable of serious discussion or thought. And so they were 'protected' from such responsibilities as voting or owning property.

Mary Wollstonecraft

Mary Wollstonecraft was probably the first woman to demand votes for women publicly – 136 years before this was achieved. Her book, *Vindication of the Rights of Women*, was published in 1792. Wollstonecraft believed women without a vote were 'women without a voice'. They had no say in the laws passed by Parliament and therefore in the way the country was run. Her book was not only about the right to vote. She challenged many of the ideas of her time. She argued for equal education for girls and boys, and for the right for single women to earn their own living. In particular she disagreed with a Frenchman called Rousseau. His ideas about education were very important at the time. Rousseau said that women were naturally inferior to men and 'ought to be weak and passive'.

> 'To please men, to be useful to them, to win their love and respect ... these are women's duties in all ages and these are what they should be taught from childhood on.'   (Rousseau)

Between 1760 and 1830 England underwent an 'Industrial Revolution'. This caused changes in the pattern of work for men and women. Work moved out of the home into the factory, so it became harder for women with young children to earn money.

THE ACCOMPLISHED WIFE AND THE BORED HUSBAND

Higher up the social scale, as the Industrial Revolution progressed, men's and women's interests became increasingly separate. Men went out into the world of business and politics. Wives were expected to stay at home and confine themselves to domestic duties and social graces – playing music, for example.

Wollstonecraft said that women should be strong, in mind and body. She felt that women were caught in a vicious circle. They were not given the same opportunities as men to develop their minds, so they appeared foolish by comparison. This, of course, seemed to prove men's point that women were naturally unintelligent and therefore not worth educating.

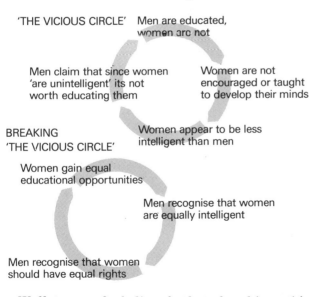

'THE VICIOUS CIRCLE' Men are educated, women are not

Men claim that since women 'are unintelligent' its not worth educating them

Women are not encouraged or taught to develop their minds

BREAKING 'THE VICIOUS CIRCLE'

Women appear to be less intelligent than men

Women gain equal educational opportunities

Men recognise that women are equally intelligent

Men recognise that women should have equal rights

Wollstonecraft believed that breaking this vicious circle would lead to many improvements in women's status. She believed that women would be allowed equal rights as soon as men recognised they were equally intelligent. Yet over a hundred years later, many of the women demanding the vote were still campaigning for the right to have the same education as men.

1. **Why did Wollstonecraft believe it was important for women to have the vote?**

2. **Why did Wollstonecraft believe that giving women equal educational opportunities was so important?**

Wollstonecraft was a brave woman. Not only did she fight hard to get her ideas taken seriously, but she suffered much personal unhappiness. She had a daughter by a man who gave her little support. At one point she attempted suicide. She later married William Godwin but died some 10 days after the birth of her second daughter. Throughout her life, and afterwards, Wollstonecraft's personal affairs overshadowed her work. She was insulted and criticised. People discussing her work have often paid more attention to her private life than her ideas. She was dismissed by many as being 'uncontrolled' and involved in 'a curious tangle of relationships'. It was not just men who condemned her. Even those suffragettes who later began to recognise just how brave and important a step she had taken for the rights of women, complained about her 'messy' private life. Others thought this was *hypocritical*, and pointed out that people rarely use events in a man's personal life as a way of criticising his work and ideas.

3. **Explain this statement in your own words.**

'We have had enough women sacrificed to this sentimental, hypocritical *prating* about purity. . . . This is one of man's most effective *engines* for our division and subjugation. . . . We have crucified the Mary Wollstonecrafts . . . of all ages.'
(Elizabeth Cady Stanton, 1815–1902)

Certain historical circumstances, such as war, can help to change the status of women by giving them opportunities to demonstrate their equality with men. Throughout history, such changes have been *accelerated* by the activities of individual women who have influenced people's views, at the time or later. Mary Wollstonecraft was one of those women. As we shall see, the nineteenth century produced many more, the majority of whom were middle class and relatively well-off. Yet without the support, determination and hard work of ordinary women, precious little change would have taken place.

Chapter 5   Fashionable Ladies

THE HAUNTED LADY, OR "THE GHOST" IN THE LOOKING-GLASS.

Clothes for rich Victorian women were heavy and elaborate. They were sewn by very poor women. In the Punch cartoon above, what point is the artist making?

Wollstonecraft died in 1797, just before the beginning of the century which was to see considerable changes in the status of women. However, none of these changes came easily. Women held meetings and marches, wrote pamphlets, gave speeches, collected signatures, *lobbied* Parliament and campaigned tirelessly. They suffered pain, hardship, ridicule, imprisonment, forced feeding and even death in order to win rights.

The nineteenth century was dominated by one particular woman: Queen Victoria. She was a highly respected monarch, who ruled for 64 years (1837–1901), yet the fact that there was a woman

Getting dressed in the era of the crinoline (hooped petticoats).

on the throne did not mean it was an age which favoured women. Indeed, the Victorian era was in many respects one of the most stifling for women – literally as well as in terms of freedom. Women's fashions changed from the loose and light garments of the eighteenth century. Tight corsets, huge crinolines and layers of heavy underskirts made movement difficult. Sleeves were long, necks high, dresses full-length. Women were more covered up than they had been for centuries. Hair was elaborately styled. Young girls had their hair tied into rag curlers every night.

The 'feminine virtues'

Pale faces and a delicate *constitution* were prized. In fact, the often boring and rather unhealthy lifestyle of middle class Victorian women and girls did seem to produce many sickly and *listless* women. They were not encouraged to exercise their bodies or their minds. The Victorian ideal was that wives should be 'ladies of leisure'. For one thing, the more servants a woman had, the more it displayed her husband's wealth. An idle wife was a sort of status symbol, as a large house or expensive car might be today.

Comics and magazines for girls reinforced these ideas. They were meant to be 'improving' as well as entertaining. Many stories encouraged the Victorian view of women as gentle and obedient, serving and supporting the men in their lives. *Holiday House*, a novel written in 1839, tells the story of Harry and Laura and their nurse's attempts to make them 'good'. While Harry is busy burning down part of the house, Laura grabs the scissors and cuts off her hated ringlets.

> ' "I was quite as naughty as Harry ..." says Laura. "I was cutting off my hair with Mrs Crabtree's scissors all the time he was setting the nursery on fire."

Later, she and Harry come face to face with a mad bull.

> 'Laura's knees tottered under her, and she instantly dropped to the ground with terror.... Harry felt quite differently, for he was a bold boy.'

1.   **Why do you think Laura chose to cut off her hair? She says this was 'quite as naughty' as setting the nursery on fire. Do you agree? When**

Harry and Laura meet the bull, what messages does the writer put across about the behaviour of girls and boys?

Earning a living

Women who did not marry were made to feel misfits. Single women were looked down upon and sometimes treated with contempt. They had none of the status a bachelor had. They had none of his independence, fun, or employment prospects.

2. Write down a list of words describing the qualities you associate with the words (a) spinster and (b) bachelor. Look at your selection and those of your friends. Are there more complimentary words in (a) or (b)? Why do you think this is?

If a genteel unmarried girl happened to be poor, because her father died leaving nothing to support her, earning her own living was very difficult. Often the only option was to become a governess, teaching the children of a wealthy family. Most governesses led fairly miserable lives. They were underpaid, undervalued and usually very lonely. They were not part of the family they served, but their social class made it hard for them to join in with the other 'family' in the household: the servants.

Society encouraged the notion that women had neither the brains nor the strength to do any of the jobs men did. Girls were meant to think of themselves as too frail to cope with anything very strenuous. Yet at the same time, thousands of working class women were proving just how much of a fiction this 'fact' was.

Throughout the nineteenth century, women worked in mines, factories, mills and on the land. They carried heavy weights and did hard and sometimes dangerous jobs. The working class woman was no lady of leisure; she hardly knew what leisure was. One woman, describing her mother's life in Victorian times, explained how her mother never had a moment to herself:

'It was bed and work all the time in those days. . . . She used to get up at 5.45 . . . then off to work . . . the housework was done in the evening . . . the baking was done at night.'

By contrast, this is Florence Nightingale's description of her life as a young well-to-do girl:

'. . . What have I done this fortnight? I have read the "Daughter at Home" to Father and two chapters of Macintosh; a volume of Sybil to Mama.

Learnt seven tunes by heart. Written various letters. Ridden with Papa. Paid eight visits. Done company. And that is all.'

In fact, Nightingale hated her idle life, in which every hour was frittered away on 'trivial tasks'.

'Women never have half an hour in all their lives (excepting before or after anyone is up . . .) that they can call their own, without fear of hurting or offending anyone.'

3. Describe the differences in daily tasks between the two lifestyles described. Is there anything they have in common?

4. Look carefully at this drawing. Why does the artist show the governess ringing the servants' bell? Does the picture give you the feeling that her life is a happy one? List five words which seem to you to describe the governess.

THE DAILY GOVERNESS

Chapter 6 Working Women

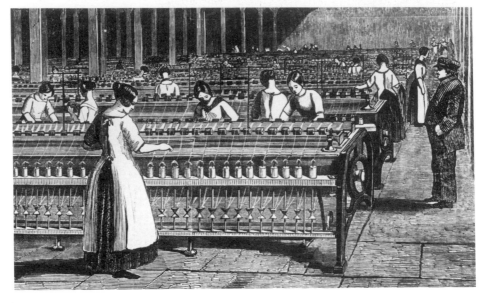

By the nineteenth century, the spinning and weaving of cloth – woollen, cotton and silk – had become one of Britain's most important industries. Women made up three-quarters of the workforce. In this picture, who is doing the work and who is supervising?

In the nineteenth century, working class men rarely earned enough to look after their families. So most poor women worked as well – as did their children. They did a lot of the farming work, including gathering the harvest after the men had cut it. They also had the backbreaking task of gleaning – this meant bending low over the fields, picking up any loose ears of grain which had dropped from the cut sheaves. Women's work was often that which was done by hand, such as weeding, picking hops and fruit, gathering vegetables etc. The overseers and farm managers were always men and on better wages. The work was often hard but farm workers generally enjoyed more freedom than factory workers.

> 'The gleaning was women's work. The men never did it. You used to get a good bit of money for it. I used to glean with my mother. But I didn't like it. She'd shout at me "Stoop your lazy back." We used to walk miles because there weren't any cornfields actually near the house.'   (Gladys Otterspoor)

> 'That was our summer holiday, it was gone gleaning. Mother used to go and take all us children, the bigger ones looked after the little ones in the field . . . we'd be sitting with the older women until the bell rang, and I was sorry sometimes to start gleaning, because the best part was before, listening to the older women's stories. The [gleaned corn would] be our flour for the year. Or we'd sell it and that had to pay the rent.'
> (Mary Coe, *Fenwomen*)

Industrial work

By the end of the century, the growth of Britain's industry had meant that the majority of the population had moved to the cities, where there were more jobs. Many women worked in the textile mills. They usually did the bulk of the work and were supervised by men, who earned higher wages. Even when men and women did the same work, women were paid less.

---

1.   Using the information in Chapter 4, explain why employers felt women should be paid lower wages than the men.

The women were usually more strictly controlled too. There were all sorts of rules and regulations. Some factory owners even fined people for talking, whistling or singing while they worked.

> 'We daren't talk and we daren't laugh. If we laughed or if we talked we had to leave off. . . . We had to sit on our stools and wait half an hour. And then we'd start work again.'
> (Flo Mellish, *Bristol As We Remember It*)

Some of the heavier jobs which women did were working in salt and coal mines. There were women brickworkers and chainmakers. They

Women did heavy, dirty and sometimes dangerous work in the Victorian mining, brick and iron industries.

carried great weights, stoked blazing furnaces, hauled coal underground – in fact, did the kind of work that richer women were told their sex was physically incapable of. There were dust-women, who collected horse manure from city streets, and 'mudlarks', who collected bits of coal which had fallen from river barges and washed up on to the muddy river banks.

At the end of a working day, most women had to cook, clean, mend clothes and take care of the family. When their children were small, it was often impossible for women to go out to work. Many of them worked alone at home, for example taking in laundry, sewing clothes or making matchboxes. These homeworkers were very poorly paid. But they needed work at any price and they were isolated in the home, so they could not band together with other workers to demand better conditions. This sort of piece-work, for which they were paid according to the amount they did, was known as 'sweated labour'. Many of

A Punch cartoon commenting on 'sweated labour' and the contrast between rich and poor (1878).

DOLLMAKERS   DOLLBREAKERS

the beautiful clothes worn by the wealthy were sewn by women who had scarcely enough to eat and whose eyes and fingers were ruined by the endless stitching.

2. In what ways were conditions for homeworkers worse than those for factory employees? Give reasons.

Domestic service

By the end of the nineteenth century domestic service had become another major form of employment for women. Behind every middle and upper class 'lady of leisure' was an army of servants. By the 1880s and 1890s one out of every three unmarried women was a servant. Some were part of a large household with lots of other servants; others were alone and responsible for everything. Some employers looked after their staff well, others did not. It was considered a 'respectable' job and good training for marriage. Employers often controlled their servants strictly and would not allow them to have boyfriends.

'Middle class people certainly had their pound of flesh in those days. Up at 6.30 in the morning, I never got to bed much before 10 at night. My time off was Wednesdays from 3 to 9.30, and on one Sunday in every month, after the mid-day dinner.'
(*Girls Are Powerful*)

'I went into the vicarage here, in service, as soon as I left school. With all that work I felt like a lady. . . . You dress nice with a white apron on, you see. White cap. Oh, it was ever so smart. . . . We was always at work. The only time we had off was a little while in the evening after tea, until we were preparing supper.'   (Sybil Hayhoe)

'We had good food, I'll say that for them. . . . But we worked hard.'   (Lily Levitt)

'I loathed the idea of going to work for someone. Because in those days you wore caps and aprons and I always felt there was something in me that I couldn't do it – I couldn't bear to be a maid to somebody. Open the door. "Yes Ma'am". Oh no, even [potato picking] was a freedom, compared to that.'   (Marjory Reeves, *Fenwomen*)

3. Look at these four quotes. What seem to be the advantages and disadvantages of domestic service?

4. Why did the last speaker prefer hard agricultural work to domestic service?

Chapter 7 The Right to Own

Caroline Norton was a successful writer. She wrote poetry, fiction and edited a magazine, yet as a married woman she had no legal right to her own earnings.

Although life for wealthy women was very different to that of overworked poor women in Victorian times, they had one thing in common. They had no legal status. A married woman's earnings automatically belonged to her husband. Her property and goods all belonged to her husband. He owned the house and any land, even if she had inherited it, and he could do what he liked with it. Of course, many poor people hardly owned a few sticks of furniture, let alone a house or some land, but the law affected them as well because it meant that any 'poor relief' or 'dole' money was paid to the man of the family, which did not necessarily mean that it reached his wife and children.

A woman could not vote. She could not go to university and take a degree. She could not get a divorce on the grounds of adultery alone, as her husband could. In fact, it was almost impossible for a woman to get a divorce at all until 1857. Even a woman's children belonged to her husband. The law said that children had only one parent, the father. He could decide where and how they were to be educated. If a couple separated, the husband could take the children and refuse to let the mother even see them.

Caroline Norton

Caroline Norton was one woman to whom this happened. Her experience made her fight for changes in the law. She was the granddaughter of the famous playwright Richard Sheridan. She was born in 1808 and she married George Norton, a lawyer and Member of Parliament, in 1827. Caroline, like her grandfather, was a talented writer. Her earnings were important because George had financial problems.

George treated his wife badly. He brought a court case claiming that Caroline had had a love affair with Lord Melbourne, an important politician. Because Caroline had no legal status, she could not even stand up in court and say one word in her defence. When the couple separated because of his brutal behaviour, Caroline found

When she married, a woman signed away her right to own. Property, money, goods and even her children belonged to her husband. Caroline Norton was one woman who fought these laws.

that he had the power to keep her three young sons away from her. Later, when she had to support herself, she discovered that he had the right to take all her earnings. She was horrified by the powerlessness of married women. She began fighting to change the law.

Many men had justified these laws by explaining that they were for women's 'protection', by giving the man the burden of dealing with all legal and financial matters. Caroline replied that she did not deny that she was 'inferior' to her husband, but pleaded:

'Put me then – (my ambition extends no further) – in the same position as all his other inferiors! In that of his housekeeper, whom he could not *libel* with *impunity* . . . of an apprentice whom he could not treat lawlessly . . . of a *scullion*, whose wages he could not refuse . . .'

(*Letter to the Queen*, 1855)

---

1. Read this extract. (a) Is Caroline Norton saying she is better or worse off than her husband's housekeeper, apprentice and scullion? (b) What incidents in her marriage is she referring to when she (i) mentions 'libel' and (ii) refers to the scullion's wages?

Some say that Caroline Norton was being *ironic* when she agreed that women were inferior because it helped her make this clever argument without angering men too much. Others say that she really did believe in her inferiority and that she wanted justice but not equal rights.

A pamphlet Caroline wrote about the Infants Custody Bill did have some effect. In 1839 the Bill was passed. It said that children under seven could stay with their mother **if** the courts agreed that the mother was of 'good character'. She wrote other important pamphlets, in which she argued in favour of changing the divorce laws so that they were fairer to women.

Barbara Bodichon

Barbara Bodichon was also tirelessly working for this cause. She wrote pamphlets and collected hundreds of signatures supporting a Married Women's Property Bill in 1856. Her aim was equal rights. She did not believe women were inferior to men. Nor was her campaign prompted by personal experience. She was happily married and wealthy in her own right, because she had a rich father who – very unusually – wished to treat his daughters the same as his sons.

2. Copy the statements and the symbols below on to a sheet of paper. As you complete this book, write down the dates and describe the Acts and events which changed these six facts about women's status at the beginning of the nineteenth century.

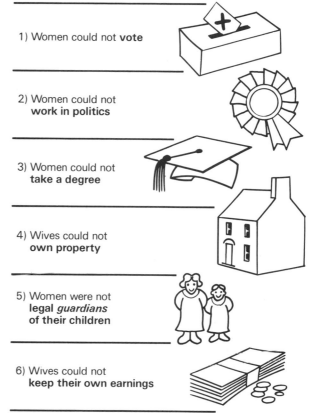

1) Women could not **vote**

2) Women could not **work in politics**

3) Women could not **take a degree**

4) Wives could not **own property**

5) Women were not legal *guardians* of their children

6) Wives could not **keep their own earnings**

---

3. Using the information in this chapter and the box below, describe how the situation for married women changed between the time Caroline Sheridan married and 1886.

1857: Matrimonial Causes Act:
allows a wife deserted by her husband to keep any money she earns. A wife separated from her husband could take legal action on her own behalf.
1870: Married Woman's Property Act:
allows women living with their husbands to keep their earnings.
1882: Married Woman's Property Act:
gives married women the same rights as unmarried. A wife could own property and give it to whoever she wished.
1886: Guardianship of Infants Act:
mothers become legal parents of their children if the father dies.
1886: Married Women (maintenance) Act:
a man who deserts his wife has to pay towards her keep.

Chapter 8   The Right to Vote

Mary Wollstonecraft was a middle class intellectual. Caroline Norton was a woman in top society. But the fight for the right to vote really got underway through the efforts of ordinary working women who campaigned with their men during the early nineteenth century.

Working people had few rights. Hours were long and wages low. There were few health and safety regulations to protect them. Employees were beginning to join together in trade unions so that they were in a stronger position to bargain for better conditions. Yet many believed that without the vote they had little chance of persuading Parliament to improve their working and living standards.

1.   Why do you think it was possible for employers to enforce such strict rules and fines on the workers?

2.   Why did working people feel gaining the vote was so important if they were to improve their living and working conditions?

Suffrage

Britain's voting system in the early nineteenth century had remained largely unchanged since medieval times. It gave voting powers to the large landowners ('householders'), who were the most powerful people. The majority of these were men, though there were a few unmarried women and widows who qualified as 'householders' because they had inherited land. But by the end of the eighteenth century, Britain was no longer a largely agricultural society. The rich landowners were outnumbered by a growing middle class of industrialists and tradespeople who owned the factories, mills, mines and businesses that were now doing so well. Although they paid as much tax as the landowners, they had no vote. The growing industrial towns often had no one to represent them in Parliament either. People complained about the unfair voting system and began to *campaign* for Parliamentary reforms. In 1832 Parliament passed a Bill which said that 'men' paying rates or rent of more than a certain value could vote. This was fairer in the sense that many more middle class men got the vote. However, no working class people qualified – and all women were now excluded.

3.   How did the Industrial Revolution show up how unfair and outdated Britain's voting system was?

4.   In what way did the 1832 Reform Bill leave women in a worse position than before?

After the disappointment of the 1832 Bill, working people fought even harder for the vote. One important movement was that of the Chartists. Another was the Co-operative Movement. In 1825 a leading Co-operator called William Thompson published *An Appeal of One Half of the Human Race, Women, against the Pretensions of the Other Half, Men.* He said that most of the ideas and experiences it described were those of his collaborator, Mrs Wheeler. He stressed the importance of women's work in the Co-operative movement. Thompson and Wheeler were particularly anxious that the fight for suffrage was in fact concentrating on votes for men. Women's suffrage had been debated in Parliament in 1797 but most people agreed with Charles James Fox, an MP. He said women would simply vote as their husbands or fathers told them, so therefore it wasn't worth giving them the vote.

A Chartist meeting in London. They were an important working class group fighting for the right to vote. This picture shows women on the speaking platform.

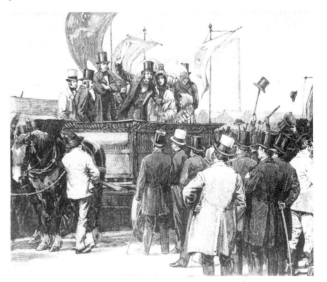

A meeting of the Co-operative Society, in which women played an active part. Co-operators own their property and goods jointly and share the profits from their work. They supported giving the vote to working people.

Here are five other arguments against giving women the vote that were put forward:
1) Women are incapable of *rational* thought.
2) Women are physically too weak and frail to take on such a burden of decision and thought.
3) Women are too *incapacitated* by frequent child-bearing to bother with the vote.
4) Women's husbands and fathers have their best interests at heart and will make the right decisions for them, so women don't need a separate vote.
5) If women have the vote they will upset the existing order of society and cause all sorts of unpleasant changes.

---

5.   In pairs or small groups discuss and prepare your own answers to the six arguments against giving women the vote.

Thompson and Wheeler also argued that women themselves had some responsibility for their low status. They had been treated like 'slaves' for so long that they unconsciously behaved like them.

> 'Awake, arise, shake off these *fetters*. Acquire the mental power of seeing them, and they are loosened for ever. Their magic depends on your ignorance, on your submission ... To obtain equal rights ... you must be respected by [men]; not merely desired, like rare meats, to *pamper* their selfish appetites. To be respected by them, you must be respectable in your own eyes; you must exert more power ... assert your right as human beings to equal individual liberty, to equal laws, political, civil, and criminal, to equal morals, to equal education – and, as a result of the whole, to equal chances.'

---

6.   (a) Do the writers lay all the blame for women's position on men?
(b) Do you think their criticism was a fair one?
(c) What do they say women must do?
(d) Rewrite this extract in your own words.

Chapter 9 Steps Forward

Thompson and Wheeler were mostly ignored or laughed at, just as Mary Wollstonecraft had been treated thirty years earlier. In 1869, another book was written arguing the case for women's rights. It was *The Subjection of Women* by John Stuart Mill, an MP. Barbara Bodichon and others working for women's suffrage had supported his election to Parliament in 1865. At last they had an ally in a position of power.

> 'Marriage is the only actual *bondage* known to our law. There remains no legal slave, except the mistress of every house.'
> (John Stuart Mill, *The Subjection of Women*, 1869)

---

1. What were the legal rights of married women at the time John Stuart Mill was writing? Do you agree with this statement? Explain your answer.

In 1867 a new Reform Bill gave the vote to the majority of working men. Women gained nothing. Mill had fought hard to replace the word 'man' with 'person' in the Bill, so that it would include some women. Although he was unsuccessful, he did manage to persuade 73 MPs to support the idea against the 194 who rejected it.

During this time local committees had been set up all over the country to fight for votes for women. Lydia Becker was one of the main leaders of the movement. She patiently organised meetings, and sent letters and petitions to persuade people of the rights of their case. A court case was fought and lost. Several Suffrage Bills were drafted and rejected. The vote remained firmly out of reach.

Between 1877 and 1878 the suffragettes held 1300 meetings. They presented 9563 petitions to Parliament with nearly 3 million signatures on them, supporting women's right to vote.

Local politics

However, women did gain some political powers. Between 1869 and the 1907 Qualification of Women Act they gained the right to vote for, and to become members of, local councils, School *Boards* and Poor Law Boards (which looked after the poor and unemployed). Thus women were in the strange position of being able to *administer* the country's laws but not having any responsibility for making them. Education, housing and the protection of children were some of the issues on which these early female politicians worked. They proved they were quite capable of dealing with political matters. In several regions, there were more women holding 'elective office' in the 1900s than the 1980s!

---

2. Look at the Time Chart. Pick out three changes in women's status and freedom which occurred between 1870 and 1907. Imagine you were alive then and write a letter to a friend describing these changes and what you feel is important about them.

Pioneers

As well as the politicians, other women were breaking new ground. Emily Davies and others were working hard to improve the opportunities for education for women (Chapter 12). Josephine Butler was waging a campaign against the unfair laws about prostitution (Chapter 14). Florence Nightingale was opening up women's opportunities for paid employment by establishing nursing as a respectable profession. She felt it was vital that middle class women had the choice of a future other than marriage. Without any chance of employment, single women and widows were condemned to poverty or dependence on others.

> 'It will be years before you obtain the suffrage for women, and in the meantime there are evils which press so much more hardly on women than the want of the suffrage.'   (Florence Nightingale)

---

3. What right did Nightingale think was more urgent than the right to vote?

Nightingale had been driven to despair by the emptiness of the idle life with which a girl of good

Elizabeth Garrett Anderson was the country's first woman doctor but she had to take her exams in Paris. She was elected on to the London School Board by more votes than any of her male rivals and in 1908 she became the first lady mayor in Britain.

family was meant to be satisfied. Eventually she persuaded her parents to let her do some hospital work. In 1854 her growing reputation and her family's good connections led to an invitation to head the nursing team sent out to improve the care of British soldiers in the Crimean War. Nightingale transformed the terrible conditions and returned a heroine. She went on to reform the nursing profession and to advise the government on this and other matters.

Mary Seacole was another nurse who showed great bravery and skill in the Crimea. She did not, however, have Nightingale's background. She was half Jamaican and her offer of service was rejected by the War Office. Seacole went anyway, and her work for the wounded soldiers won her such praise that she was awarded two medals. Later, her name was forgotten and her work became completely overshadowed by that of the more socially acceptable Nightingale.

4. (a) Why do you think the War Office rejected Mary Seacole's offer to go to the Crimea? (b) Why do you think they saw Florence Nightingale as a better choice?

Although Nightingale has been remembered, it is largely as the angelic 'lady of the lamp'. In fact, she hated the idea of nurses being seen as gentle, frail creatures dabbing a fevered brow. Being a nurse meant being tough, strong and certainly not squeamish. Of course, these were not 'womanly' qualities in Victorian eyes. The myth of the 'lady of the lamp' was a more acceptable image. Yet the idea of the 'angel of the home' was exactly what Nightingale and other women working for women's rights at this time were questioning. It was a brave thing to do. Some women did not have the strength or courage to move beyond their traditional role. Some simply could not see any disadvantages in their situation. They could not see what good the vote would do them. A few actively opposed the movement to women's rights and in 1890 they formed an Anti-Suffrage League. Queen Victoria herself said,

> 'The Queen is most anxious to enlist every one who can speak or write to join in checking this mad, wicked folly of "Women's Rights".'

5. Mary Seacole has largely been ignored by history books. The most common image of Florence Nightingale is the misleading one of the 'lady of the lamp'. What does this tell us about the way history books can affect our view of women?

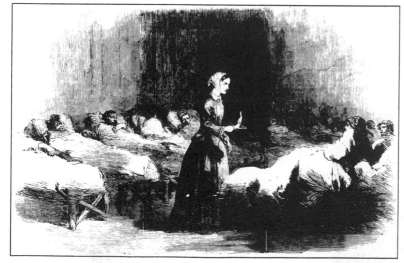

THE LADY OF THE LAMP

6. How do Nightingale's words, below, conflict with this popular picture of her?

"Any woman who takes a sentimental view of Nursing (which she calls 'ministering', as if she were an angel), is of course worse than useless." (Florence Nightingale)

Chapter 10 Winning the Vote

In 1897 the local groups working for women's votes joined together into the National Union of Women's Suffrage Societies (NUWSS). Their leader was now Millicent Garrett Fawcett. She continued Lydia Becker's method of patient argument and persuasion. Some women were beginning to lose confidence in this method. They argued that men were tricking them – 'for if we are as good as they ask us to be, then we don't cause them any trouble and there is no reason for them to take any notice of us.'

Patience or anger?

In 1903 Emmeline Pankhurst formed the Women's Social and Political Union (WSPU). Support for the WSPU grew rapidly. Its approach was quite different to that of the more peaceable NUWSS. They *picketed* minister's houses, lobbied MPs and interrupted meetings, shouting and waving banners. For some of these actions they went to prison and gained much publicity. Although Fawcett would not adopt the same methods, she did admit that 'The action of the prisoners has touched the imagination of the country in a manner quieter methods did not succeed in doing.'

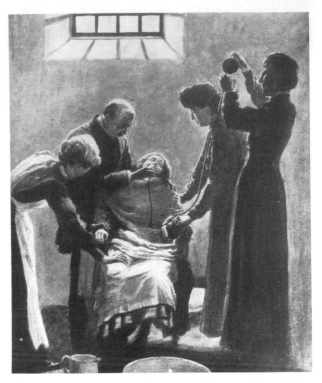

Suffragette prisoners on hunger strike were force-fed. Liquid food was forced into their stomachs through a tube.

1. Why did the WSPU want more *militant* action?

2. Did Fawcett agree that the different methods of the WSPU had helped the cause and if so, in what way?

After 1909, the WSPU stepped up the pressure. They broke windows, chained themselves to railings, wrote slogans on walls and fought back at the policemen who arrested them. Some of the imprisoned women started hunger striking. The Government decided they should be force-fed. It

The militant actions of the WSPU led to many arrests.

was a horribly painful and sometimes dangerous process. In 1913 the Government tried another plan. They would release the starving women and then arrest them again as soon as they were well, 'playing' with them like a cat with a mouse.

3. Why was the Government's action of 1913 known as the Cat and Mouse Act?

4. Design a poster protesting against either the Cat and Mouse Act or forcible feeding.

5. Make two lists describing the advantages and disadvantages of (a) peaceful protest and (b) more violent methods. Then divide into groups representing the NUWSS and the WSPU. Debate the value of these different methods of campaign.

In 1910 a Parliamentary Committee was formed to settle the matter. Women had high hopes of a solution. The Committee proposed the Conciliation Bill. To conciliate means to solve disagreements. The Bill went through various stages but in 1911 the Liberal Prime Minister, Asquith, announced that he was putting up another Reform Bill, which would give all men the vote. Many MPs thought this was more important. This caused them to withdraw support for the Conciliation Bill, which was then defeated. This was a terrible blow to the suffragettes.

The war effort

Nevertheless, they went on campaigning until World War One broke out in 1914. Even though the suffragette organisations had been badly let down by the Liberal Government, they felt their duty was now to support it. They turned their skill and energy towards encouraging women to help in the war effort. They proved to be a highly effective workforce. Suddenly the press and politicians started praising women, saying 'The nation is grateful'. The *Daily Mail* began to support their claim for the vote and gave their war work lots of publicity. Of course, many poor women had been doing hard physical work before the war but nobody had ever taken much notice.

'The cause of votes for women would be safe, provided our country and its constitution were preserved.'   (Christabel Pankhurst)

'We rallied to our country, not its particular Government.'   (Emmeline Pankhurst)

---

6.   What reasons do Emmeline Pankhurst and her daughter give for supporting the Government during the war?

Women for peace

Not all women wanted to help the war effort. Some felt deeply that war of any kind was wrong.

During the First World War, women drove buses and trains, worked in arms factories, became farmers, plumbers and electricians and did other 'male' jobs.

Emmeline Pankhurst's second daughter, Sylvia, was one of a group of people who opposed the war. They tried to persuade the politicians to search for peaceful ways of dealing with Europe's problems. In 1915 two thousand brave women from all over Europe and North America met together in Holland for an International Congress for Peace.

The war dragged on. Out of all the suffering came at least one good thing. Politicians could no longer argue that women had no minds of their own, no political understanding and no role to play in the nation. In 1918 the Coalition Government, made up of Liberal, Conservative and Labour politicians, gave all men over 21 and all women over 30 the vote. The same year the war ended.

---

7.   Thousands of men were killed during the First World War. Can you think why the politicians decided only women over the age of 30 could vote?

---

8.   Look at the Time Chart. In how many other nations and states had women won the vote before they did in Britain?

In 1928 women at last got the vote on equal terms with men. It was called the 'flapper vote' because fashionable young girls in the 1920s were known as 'flappers'. Some men had objected to them having the vote because they said they were too frivolous. Yet the struggle to win the vote had shown that women were not interested only in domestic or frivolous matters. What is more, they were prepared to suffer ridicule and imprisonment in order to fulfil those wider interests. Winning the vote at last gave a women a voice in the way the country was governed.

---

9.   What does this statement mean? In groups discuss whether you agree with it.

'The struggle for the vote was more important then the result. It was not the vote which liberated the suffragettes but the discovery of strength and determination which they never knew they possessed.'

---

10.   Look at the Time Chart. How many years after women got the vote on equal terms with men was a law passed which gave them equal pay? Why do you think this was so?

Chapter 11 Education for Life

This drawing makes fun of early nineteenth century schools where rich young ladies learnt 'graceful attitudes' and good posture. One pupil complained "Everything was taught to us in inverse ratio of its importance. At the bottom were Morals and Religion – and at the top Music and Dancing – miserably poor music too."

What does the girl mean by saying that they were taught everything in 'inverse ratio' of its importance?

Women knew that winning the vote was just a beginning. The vote gave them a voice in political matters, but without education few women would have the confidence or skills to use that voice and speak out. While the suffragettes were fighting for the vote, others were fighting for equal educational opportunities.

Until the end of the nineteenth century, education for most girls had one end in view: domesticity. The only difference was that wealthy girls were being educated to be domestic angels and poor girls to be domestic drudges. And as long as women – rich or poor – were brought up to believe that their role in life was to be wives and mothers, it was going to be hard for the majority to do anything else.

Here is the comment of a woman writing in 1869 on the situation for well-to-do girls. They were taught 'drawing room' skills such as embroidery, piano playing and dancing which would attract a husband. They were not encouraged to use their minds.

> 'Hence proceed many unhappy marriages, when the bride only flees to marriage to save her from the *insipid* uselessness of her life.'
>
> (Penelope Holland, *Macmillan Magazine*)

Domestic drudge

At the beginning of the nineteenth century, most schools for the poor were run by religious groups or charities. Many working class children did not have much chance to go to school. They started work as young as eight years old. As Britain's trade and industry developed, the need for skilled and literate workers grew. The government began to realise that a poorly educated workforce was a disadvantage. Britain was beginning to lag behind its competitors in the world market place. Parliament passed laws which reduced the number of hours children could be made to work. And in 1870 an Education Act was approved which stated that all local authorities should provide schools.

Many children still missed lessons at the new *Board Schools*. Their parents could not do without their earnings and their help at home. Girls tended to miss out most, as this school log book tells us:

> 'May and June 1891: Irregular attendance. Out of 29 children absent, 21 were girls.'   (*Fenwomen*)

Girls had to look after their younger brothers and sisters almost as soon as they could hold a baby.

They had to help their mothers with time-consuming household chores.

'When I think of my mother's washing day for the family once a week, that was a day's hard labour.... We went down two flights of stairs to a horrible dark backyard washing-house. You had to light the fire in the boiler to get the water boiling for the washing. There were horrible old tubs and a grimy old wash-house that nobody really cared about because eight families used it.'

(Annie Davison, *Dutiful Daughters*)

1. **What does this account of washday tell us about housework in the 1900s?**

2. **Why did girls from poor families miss school so often?**

When they did attend school, children were taught handicrafts, as well as the 'three Rs' – reading, writing and 'rithmetic. The boys learnt crafts such as carpentry, aimed at getting them a job. The girls were taught domestic skills, such as sewing and laundrywork, aimed at making them good housewives.

Learning domestic work in a London school, 1908.

3. (a) **In what way did the subjects learnt by poor girls differ from those taught to the rich?**
(b) **In what way was the purpose of their education similar?**

4. **Poor girls were educated to be 'wives to the poor' and 'servants to the rich'. Do you think this a fair description?**

The movement for better education challenged the place of women in society. It questioned the idea that women's sole ambition should be to support the men in their lives and look after the home. These are some of the arguments people used against it:

'There is no question . . . that the mind of woman is or ever can be equal to that of man.'

'Giving them a boy's education will damage their reproductive organs.'

'a new race' of educated women 'will destroy the grace and charm of social life.'

'Profoundly educated women rarely make good wives or mothers.'

5. **Write out these statements at the top of four columns. Are any of them presented as though they are facts? How many are opinions? Write the answer to this in each column, followed by a few sentences of reply to each one.**

It was not only men who argued against educating women. Many women were equally convinced of their mental inferiority. As Mary Wollstonecraft had pointed out, if girls' heads are filled only with silly and foolish ideas, they will grow up ignorant. Thus they will seem to prove, to themselves and others, the theory that they are unintelligent. Some women did support the idea of improved education but only in order that they could be better wives and mothers. They did not see it as a means to their own fulfilment or independence.

6. **How does Wollstonecraft explain the fact that many women appeared to be unintelligent? Is 'ignorant' the same as 'unintelligent'? Use them in a sentence to show you understand their meaning.**

7. **Using the information on education in Chapter 3, as well as Nightingale's comment on her life as a young lady in Chapter 5 and the picture and quote opposite, prepare a short talk on how the quality of women's education affected their ambitions and their status in society. (Use the following questions to help you: Were women educated – to be independent; to earn their own living; to take part in politics; to be men's equal in conversation and learning; to think for themselves; to be charming and decorative; to be wives and mothers; to challenge ideas?)**

Chapter 12   The Right to Learn

The laboratory, Girton College, Cambridge. The first women students were expected to behave very well and were always accompanied by an older woman when they went for walks or to their lectures.

As long as middle class women had virtually no chance of earning their own money and were therefore financially dependent on their husbands and as long as working class women could only earn very low wages, the alternatives to marriage were not attractive. The right to education was linked with the right to work. A poorly educated woman had little chance of getting a good job.

---

1.   'No pay or low pay made marriage almost compulsory.' Discuss in groups the meaning of this statement and decide if you agree with it.

Redundant women

During the nineteenth century, women in Britain gradually outnumbered men. Some men had died in war. Others had emigrated. Others simply didn't want to marry. A bachelor had a good life, unlike spinsters who had so little freedom or earning power. By 1860 about one in four women were unlikely to find a husband. Yet there were no universities, teacher training colleges, trade or technical schools where they were allowed to learn skills to support themselves. In 1862 one man proposed a solution to this problem of 'redundant women', as he called them.

'There is an enormous and increasing number of single women ... who, in place of completing, sweetening and *embellishing* the existence of others, are compelled to lead an independent and incomplete existence of their own.... Women who live in and by their intelligence alone ... are abnormal and not perfect natures.'

His main suggestion was that about half a million women should be shipped off to the colonies or the United States, where they might find husbands. He also approved of the rising numbers of domestic servants.

'Female servants ... are fully and usefully employed ... they embellish, *facilitate*, and serve. In a word, they fulfill both essentials of a woman's being: they are supported by, and they *minister* to, men.' (W. R. Greg, 'Why Are Women Redundant')

---

2.   Greg's essay was reprinted and seriously discussed many times in the 1860s.
(a) What are the two sources of support for women which he approves of?   (b) What does he regard as women's 'essential' role in life?
(c) What is your opinion of his arguments?

Progress

In the nineteenth century, some very determined people took the first steps towards equal educational opportunities. In 1868 a Government report revealed the low standards of education in girls' schools. Earlier, another report had described the hopeless training and low status of governesses. In 1848 Queen's College for Women was opened and Bedford College opened one year later. In 1850 Frances Buss founded North London Collegiate School. In 1858 Dorothea Beale founded Cheltenham Ladies College. In these and other schools girls received the kind of education which prepared them for university and for work in the Civil Service or professions such as medicine or teaching.

Higher education

The opportunities for further education and training increased. Girls could go to the Nightingale School for Nurses, founded in 1860, or train as doctors at the Elizabeth Garrett Anderson Hospital where patients and staff were all women. In 1876 the government passed a law which allowed all medical schools to admit women as students. In spite of a lot of hostility from some male doctors and even from some patients, by the 1890s a number of women had qualified as doctors.

Meanwhile Emily Davies had persuaded the universities to allow girls to take the same school exams as the boys were taking. Davies always refused any offer of a special girls' exam. Some people felt that girls' education had to be improved so that it was as good as but different from that of boys, by missing out higher mathematics, Latin and Greek. Emily Davies believed that 'different means lower'. She was convinced that they had to take exactly the same exams. Otherwise, she argued, men would always be able to claim that women weren't equally intelligent. Davies and others also worked hard to get teacher training for women, for the poor standards at girls' schools were largely due to the fact that women teachers were so badly educated themselves.

Davies then tried to get universities to accept women as degree students. They refused, so she opened Hitchin College. The students were taught by professors from nearby Cambridge University. Later she moved the college to Girton. It became the first female college at Cambridge University. In 1873 the women took the same degree as the men and got excellent results. The university refused to award them diplomas but a victory had been won. They had proved that women were perfectly capable of high educational standards.

These improvements in training and education largely benefited girls whose families could afford the fees. But by the end of the nineteenth century several areas of work had opened up for less wealthy middle class girls. The telephone had been invented in 1876. Soon switchboard operators were needed. The invention of the typewriter and of *shorthand* set off a growing demand for shorthand writers and typists. The expanding middle class was eager to spend its money. Shops multiplied. Large department stores such as Selfridges opened up. They needed sales assistants, buyers and manageresses.

---

3. Why did Davies believe that a different syllabus and exam for girls would be a bad thing? Do you think she was right?

---

4. Sometimes technological change has affected the position of women in society. Choose two nineteenth-century inventions and describe how they opened up women's employment opportunities.

A London telephone exchange, 1901, staffed entirely by women.

An office scene in the early 1900s.

Chapter 13 Protection or Restriction?

Middle class women were winning the right to work. Most working class women had little choice but a lifetime of work – usually poorly paid. From the 1850s, more and more skilled male workers had joined together in trade unions to fight for improvements in wages, hours and conditions. They began to set up membership rules to protect their jobs. These had the effect of increasingly excluding women from the better paid work. The growing use of machinery meant that there was less need for sheer physical strength. Women were capable of doing more and more industrial jobs. But what tended to happen was that men kept the 'skilled' jobs of minding the machinery and supervising workers, while women got the lower paid, often exhausting work by hand.

The Factory Acts

From the beginning of the nineteenth century, a series of Factory Acts were passed which were intended to improve working conditions. They included rules directed specifically at women, eg:

Women workers in a cycle factory, Coventry. Look back to page 14. Can you see something similar about the roles of men and women in these two factory scenes?

1) Women must take their meals together, apart from the men
2) Women may not do certain kinds of work (usually skilled)
3) Women must give up work when they marry
4) Women must not work during the night
5) Women may only do limited amounts of overtime

Employers, the government and the trade unions (organisations composed almost entirely of men) said these rules were in women's interest. They said they were to 'protect' them from exploitation and from the 'corrupting' influences of factory life. The Victorians worried that young women would be led astray by mixing with men in the overcrowded factories. Their critics pointed out that these 'protective' measures were usually only applied to those trades, such as textiles, where women were in competition with men. They also objected to the way the laws treated women more as children than as equals to men.

   . . . 'the "not quite adult" status of industrial women affects the entire position of women in society. It *perpetuates* the notion that they are not quite persons; that they are not able to look after themselves. . . . Further . . . it was only in well-paid processes, where women came into competition with men, that restrictions have been thought desirable. Charwomen have no *statutory* hours for mealtimes. There is no *prohibition* of night work for domestic servants. Nurses may lift heavy weights, and working mothers continue coal-carrying and floor-scrubbing through pregnancy till the first pangs of labour.'

          (Winifred Holtby, *Women*, 1934)

1. **Sum up in your own words Winifred Holtby's argument.**

2. **She points out that jobs such as charring and domestic service were not covered by protective legislation. What explanation does she give?**

3. **Look carefully at the factory rules (left). Why do you think women complained that sometimes these rules 'restricted' rather than 'protected' them? Explain why 2 and 5 in particular might be seen as restrictive. Why do you think 1 was introduced?**

The Women's Trade Union League

After the Short Hours Bill of 1872, many women protested against the unequal restrictions which were based on a worker's sex. In 1874 the Women's Trade Union League was founded by Emma Patterson. She helped women in various trades to organise themselves into unions. Women were handicapped in several ways:

1) Household responsibilities made it hard to find time to go to meetings.
2) Lower wages meant smaller contributions to union funds.
3) The frequent belief that work was a stop-gap until marriage, discouraged them from getting involved.
4) They were not brought up to speak out for themselves.

4. Why did the fact that women were expected, and sometimes compelled, to give up work once they married put them in a weaker bargaining position with employers?

Patterson encouraged women's unions to build up funds so that they could pay members sickness and other benefits. She won a fight to have female factory inspectors in trades which employed mostly women. She opposed the Factory Bill and many of the 'protective' laws. She felt they often put women at a disadvantage, by excluding them from work they desperately needed. Although she and many of the other organisers of the movement were middle class, their work was a real attempt to meet the needs of working class women.

Attitudes about women working were slow to change. John Ruskin, who believed in social reform, wrote to Patterson saying he sympathised with her ideals but added that they were complicated 'with the infinite error of [making] the sexes independent ... men must maintain their women or they are worse than beasts.'

5. What belief about the role of men and women do Ruskin's words reveal? How does it tie in with the idea of the family wage? In groups, discuss whether you think these ideas are still widespread.

The match girls' strike

In the 1880s working women were responsible for a remarkable achievement in trade union history. In 1888 the match girls of Bryant and May's London factory led a strike. Their success encouraged not only women workers but all unskilled workers. Up to this point most unions had been for skilled men. The match girls proved that unskilled workers, however poor, could have considerable power if they united.

The match girls worked long hours for low pay. The work itself was dangerous. The girls had to dip the matches by hand into a chemical called phosphorus. This caused a painful disease called 'phossy jaw' which rotted the girls' teeth, gums and jaw bones. Annie Besant, a *socialist*, wrote about the girls in an article called 'White Slavery in London'. Besant tried to get the wealthy shareholders to imagine their own daughters suffering like the match girls. The factory management was furious but eventually they agreed to the girls' demands for better conditions and pay.

6. Find out more about the strike and write an account of it from the point of view of a match girl.

7. Why was the strike important for all unskilled workers?

The match girls' work was badly paid and bad for their health. The chemicals rotted their teeth and jaws. They also carried heavy boxes on their heads, which damaged their backs and rubbed away their hair. In 1888 they struck successfully for better conditions.

Chapter 14 Double Standards

Josephine Butler campaigned against the government's unfair laws about prostitution. She exposed the double standards which they used to justify the laws.

Birth control, employment conditions and legal rights were just some of the issues on which Annie Besant campaigned in her busy life.

The contrast between the daughters of Bryant and May's share holders and the match girls was an example of the contrast between the lives of rich and poor women which became particularly marked in the nineteenth century. Rich women were at their idlest when poor women were working hardest. Rich women were told they were too fragile to work, while working women were proving this was not true. Because working women worked alongside men to whom they were neither related nor married, they were regarded as being rather bold, rowdy and immoral. Rich women, on the other hand, were meant to be 'pure and innocent'. If their husbands were unfaithful and visited prostitutes, this was regarded as quite natural but it was considered a terrible sin if a wife had an affair.

Money and morals

Many poor working women were forced into prostitution because their wages were so low. In the 1870s the Contagious Diseases Acts were passed. They meant that a woman suspected of being a prostitute could be arrested and forced to undergo an unpleasant examination for disease.

Josephine Butler was a wealthy woman who campaigned against these laws. She pointed out the double standards in people's attitudes. First, that behaviour which was considered natural for men, was seen as wicked for women. Second, that the law punished prostitutes and not the men who 'used' them. Finally, she made the point that women became prostitutes because they needed money, not because they were 'sinful' by nature. If they were given proper training for good jobs and a decent wage when they had one, they would not need to become prostitutes. She tried to make people see the connection between money and 'morals'.

Prostitutes were imprisoned; never the men who 'used' them. Any woman suspected of being a prostitute could be forcibly examined for disease.

A PAINTED LILY IN TROUBLE

1. (a) What were the double standards Butler exposed?

(b) Discuss in pairs the quote below and whether some 'double standards' continue today.

'A boy who is sexually active is "a bit of a lad"; a girl is "a bit of a slag".'

(Teenagers in the 1980s, *The Role of Women*)

In 1886 the Acts were abolished. But many of the attitudes which lay behind them lingered on. Butler herself found that she did not always get full support from other middle class women. Partly this was because prostitution was not a 'safe' subject, like education or the vote. Many women were embarrassed or ashamed to get involved in the campaign. Victorian society frowned upon discussion about anything to do with sex. It was associated with sin and shame.

Even more important, many suffragettes felt they did not dare risk any scandal. When the suffrage movement first began to be organised in the 1850s, women felt they had to avoid giving men the slightest chance of attacking their ideas through criticism of the way they led their lives. They saw how effectively Mary Wollstonecraft's critics had attacked her, by saying her ideas were as 'messy' as her lifestyle. The generations of feminists who followed Wollstonecraft felt they had to convince society that they were respectable, moral women. They acted in the way that they thought would bring about greatest gains for women. They didn't want to put men off from taking them seriously – and they didn't want to frighten women away either.

This explains why Emily Davies was so strict with the first women university students. She knew that the authorities would be watching like hawks for the slightest evidence that education for women made them behave in a way that was considered immoral. While she and others may have approved of Butler's campaign, they dared not publicly support it, in case it endangered their work for education and suffrage.

---

2. What does this mean? Explain it in your own words.

'Mary Wollstonecraft was used to make a connection between feminism and immorality.'

---

3. How did the way Mary Wollstonecraft was treated affect the nineteenth-century feminists? Do you think the women's movement today feels the need to 'behave well' in order not to antagonise men?

Birth control

One woman who was brave enough to speak out about sexual matters in Victorian times was Annie Besant. Before she got involved in workers' rights and the match girls' strike, she had been campaigning to make information about birth control available to working women. One hundred years ago, most couples had about six children. Families of eight or ten were not uncommon. And many women gave birth to more babies who didn't survive. Women's health suffered from frequent pregnancies. Poor women could rarely afford proper medical care, time off from work or even enough food to build up their strength and health. The only contraceptives available were expensive and there was little information about them. Whatever the improvements in women's working, educational or political rights, they were hardly going to have either strength or time to take full advantage of them as long as marriage meant a succession of pregnancies.

---

4. Do you agree with this? Explain why.

'It is quite obvious that much of woman's emancipation does depend on the ability to prevent pregnancy.' (Constance Rover)

In 1877 Annie Besant and a colleague, Charles Bradlaugh, published a book about birth control at a price which working women could afford. They were arrested and put on trial. They were found guilty of publishing material likely 'to deprave public morals' but successfully appealed against this verdict. In 1885 a Dr Albutt published a book costing sixpence with information on birth control. He too was put on trial. He pointed out that it contained no facts that could not be found in books costing £2.00. Like Besant and Bradlaugh, his 'crime' was making the information available to poor people.

---

5. Imagine you are Annie Besant on trial. Using a tape recorder, make a short speech defending your action and saying why you feel it is important for poor women to have information about birth control.

Chapter 15 The Right to Choose

Marie Stopes and her nurses at the Mother's Clinic for Constructive Birth Control, London, the first such clinic in the country

In spite of the efforts of Besant and others, government and medical opposition to birth control continued. Even in the 1920s, women were still fighting to have the knowledge and the means to limit their families. Dora Russell was one woman who campaigned hard for birth control and maternity leave. She and others held mass public meetings. Thousands of women – and many men – turned up, eager for information and help. In 1921 Marie Stopes opened the first birth control clinic. In 1924 she, Dora Russell and Margaret Sanger, an American pioneer in birth control, founded the Workers Birth Control Group. They put pressure on the government and on local councils to help with clinics and information. This is one woman's description of how she and others felt at the time:

> '... so many men didn't want women to know how to control the number of children they had ... they thought they'd lose control over women if women could refuse to have children. When male doctors and lawyers get involved ... it's not the women they think of, but their own rules and regulations ... [but] it isn't a medical or legal matter, it's a women's matter.'
> (Hazel Hunkins Hallinan, 1890–1982)

Slowly the secrecy surrounding birth control was broken down. The Family Planning Association was founded in 1939, the number of clinics increased, and government organisations began to be more helpful. However, it was a long time before the state gave its full support. It was not until 1967 that all local authorities had to provide family planning services. That same year a new law was passed which made it possible to have abortions under the National Health system. However, it can still be difficult for a woman to get an abortion, particularly if her doctor disapproves. Opinion about abortion remains divided and there have been attempts to change the 1967 Act.

Since the 1950s new and more efficient methods of birth control have been developed. No method is ideal: some have side effects, others are awkward or not completely effective. But today it is

Large families were common in the Victorian era. This mother of 19 children looks remarkably well but many women's health and happiness suffered from constant pregnancies. Information about birth control was hard to get hold of, especially for the poor.

much easier for couples to choose whether and when to have children. Since 1975, *maternity leave* has to be granted. More people are recognising that looking after children is something for which both sexes should be responsible. There is a campaign for fathers to have *paternity* leave.

Pain and privilege

'Pregnancy and childbirth: the pain, the power and the privilege which *define* a woman as different from a man.... But the power of childbearing is a blessing laced with bitterness ... instead of defining just one difference between men and women, women's ability to bear children is used to define their entire lives. It is used to justify and create a role for women.'

(D. Taylor, *Women: A World Report*, 1985)

Debbie Taylor says that because women can produce children, all too often they are put into a situation where that is seen as their only ability – and other roles in society have been denied to them. In fact, at times it has seemed as though society regarded it as women's 'fault' that they produce children, rather than recognising that they are actually doing society a service.

---

1. Discuss in groups the ways in which you think women's role as mothers has affected their status in society.

Working status

The right to choose whether and when to have children was crucial to women's fight for greater equality. With more control over that aspect of their lives, they had more chance of being educated, trained, employed and financially independent. Changes in laws and attitudes have been crucial to changing women's status, but technical change has been important too. New contraceptive technology changed family planning. New technology affected women's job opportunities. The invention of factory and office machinery changed the pattern of employment. Machines took over much heavy manual work. As factories grew in size, they needed people to do the paperwork involved in buying in materials, dealing with orders, and paying the workers. Shops, banks, trading and insurance companies expanded to deal with all this increased trade. They needed people to write letters, take dictation, keep accounts, file records etc. Women took on much of this work.

Such changes were sometimes a mixed blessing. As women took over *clerical* work, its status went down. Before the typewriter was invented, paperwork was done by male clerks by hand. It was respected as skilled work. There were *promotion* prospects. The invention of more and more office machinery meant that clerical work began to be seen as mechanistic, repetitive work. In addition, because women were expected to give up work once they married, promotion to a more demanding and satisfying task was never built into the secretary's role. Men no longer undertook clerical work, because it was unlikely to lead to further responsibility. Once again, women found themselves in an often undervalued and underpaid profession.

---

2. Copy out this crossword and complete it, using Chapters 11, 12, 13, 15 and the Time Chart to help you. The number of letters in the answer is given (in brackets) at the end of each clue.

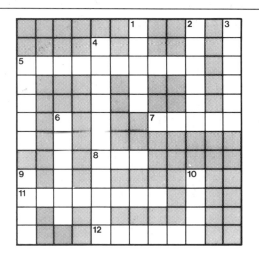

Across

5. The invention of this machine opened up a new kind of office employment for women (10)

7. ----- Besant campaigned for women workers' rights (5)

8. Some Victorians believed educated women would make --- mothers (3)

11. (See 4 down)

12. She pioneered the cause of university education for women (6)

Down

1. (See 5 down)

2. This was the first women's college at Cambridge University (6)

3. The success of this ------ in 1888 was an important victory for women and all unskilled workers (6)

4. (and 11 across) The invention of the telephone gave many women the chance of a job as a ----------- -------- (11, 8)

5. (and 1 down) An organisation which helps people gain better employment conditions (5, 5)

6. In 1873 women passed the same ------ as men (6)

9. Florence Nightingale believed women should be able to choose to ---- rather than marry (4)

10. She founded a famous school for girls in 1850 (4)

Chapter 16   War and the Depression

Women took on many so-called 'men's' jobs during World War One.

World War One accelerated the changes taking place in women's employment. Once again, historical circumstances gave women an opportunity to prove their ability in areas previously denied to them. As the war dragged on, the government needed more skilled and semi-skilled workers. They particularly needed people in the traditionally 'male' trades of engineering and metalwork, to produce the weapons of war. Women trained and took on the work. They also became farm workers, transport workers, mechanics and porters, as well as doing more traditionally 'female' jobs such as nursing. Some 400,000 women gladly left domestic service for these various jobs.

Changing attitudes

Women's effectiveness as workers during the war earned them gratitude and increased respect from the government. Women themselves found their attitudes to work changed. Those who had done men's jobs now questioned the idea that women could only do lower paid, less skilled work. Upper and middle class women who had worked for the first time in their lives now questioned the idea that it was 'unladylike' to work outside the home. Many women gained skills and confidence.

The end of the war seemed to promise many improvements. Women over the age of 30 had the vote. The Treaty of Versailles, which ended the war, officially approved the principle of equal pay for equal work. Britain's Sex Disqualification Act was passed. The number of women in trade unions was rising.

Before long, however, life was looking less promising. Many ex-servicemen were looking for work. Women were told to give up their jobs and go back into the home. A government report came out which did not approve of the principle of equal pay. The popular press changed its tune too:

'The idea that because the state called for women to help the nation, the state must continue to employ them is too absurd for serious women to entertain.'
(*Daily Graphic*)

1.   **How does this situation remind you of events during and after the Civil War? (See Chapter 3.)**

The Depression

By 1921 Britain's economy was in trouble. The following years – a period known as the Depression – brought financial problems to banks and businesses throughout Europe and America. By 1930 there were three million unemployed people in Britain. Worst hit were the 'heavy' industries, such as iron, steel and shipbuilding. These mainly employed men. The 'light' industries were expanding and employing women. However, women were badly affected by the slump in the textile industry, in which many of them worked.

Women suffered from the way the government's unemployment benefit was paid. Working people paid regular sums into a National Insurance scheme. It paid them back a small amount if they found themselves faced with unemployment or sickness. It did not, however, cover domestic servants and some other jobs. The low pay and lack of freedom of domestic service made it a last

Queuing for unemployment benefit. Although the 1920s and 30s were prosperous for some (see opposite), the same period, called the Depression, saw great poverty in many areas of England.

34

resort for most women. Yet if someone refused such a job, she was regarded as not genuinely looking for work. She lost her right to benefit. Women also received less benefit than men, although their contributions when in work were the same. The thinking behind this and other legislation was the family wage principle: men support families and women only work for 'pin money'. No distinctions were made for single men or for the thousands of women who, for one reason or another, were the family breadwinner.

Parts of Britain did well during the Depression. The new 'light' industries were based in the Midlands, the South and South East. People living in these areas had jobs and therefore money to buy the products made by these new factories: electrical goods, household furniture, radios and labour-saving devices such as vacuum cleaners and gas cookers. The health of mothers and children improved. Family planning clinics were opening up. The birth rate was beginning to fall. Childhood diseases were better understood and treated. More packaged, bottled and tinned foods became available. Yet while housekeeping became less demanding, it also became more boring and lonely. This was the beginning of the *consumer*

In the 1920s and 30s well-off women began to benefit from labour-saving machines. Manufacturers realised the importance of women consumers. Advertisements promoted the image of the perfect housewife, whose only concern was her home and family.

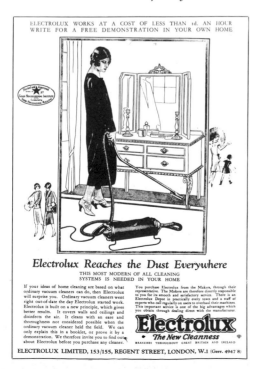

ELECTROLUX WORKS AT A COST OF LESS THAN 1d. AN HOUR
WRITE FOR A FREE DEMONSTRATION IN YOUR OWN HOME

Electrolux Reaches the Dust Everywhere
THIS MOST MODERN OF ALL CLEANING
SYSTEMS IS NEEDED IN YOUR HOME

If your ideas of home cleaning are based on what ordinary vacuum cleaners can do, then Electrolux will surprise you. Ordinary vacuum cleaners went right out-of-date the day Electrolux started work. Electrolux is built on a new principle, which gives better results. It cleans with an ease and thoroughness not considered possible when the ordinary vacuum cleaner held the field. We can only explain this in a booklet, or prove it by a demonstration. We therefore invite you to find out about Electrolux before you purchase any cleaner.

You purchase Electrolux from the Makers, through their representative. The Makers are therefore directly responsible to you for its smooth and satisfactory service. There is an Electrolux Depot in practically every town and a staff of experts who call regularly on users to overhaul their machines. This important service is one of the big advantages which you obtain through dealing direct with the manufacturer.

Electrolux
• The New Cleanness •
BRANCHES THROUGHOUT GREAT BRITAIN AND IRELAND

ELECTROLUX LIMITED, 153/155, REGENT STREET, LONDON, W.1 (Gerr. 4947 8)

age in which housewives became an ever more important market. Advertisers began to encourage women to see 'a whiter wash' or 'a cleaner carpet' as their main goal in life.

---

2. Running a household in the seventeenth century was a highly skilled job, involving nursing, teaching, producing and preserving food, spinning and weaving and other crafts. List the advantages and disadvantages that twentieth century labour-saving devices and convenience foods have brought to women's lives.

The fight goes on
Throughout this period the women's movement continued to fight for legal, social and economic rights. Conditions were difficult. The deaths of men in the war meant there were many single or widowed women, yet the government was making a great effort to get women back into the home and away from jobs and independence.

New organisations developed from the old suffrage ones, such as the National Union of the Societies for Equal Citizenship and the Townswomen's Guilds. They wanted to attract people who hadn't been involved with the women's movement before. They provided a space for women to meet, discuss ideas and exchange information, skills and experiences. There were talks on current affairs and how they affected women. The aim of these organisations was to educate women politically and encourage them to use their vote responsibly.

The Six Point Group was founded in 1921. It had six demands:
1) Satisfactory laws about child assault
2) Satisfactory laws for widowed mothers
3) Satisfactory laws for unmarried mothers and their children
4) Equal guardianship of children
5) Equal pay for teachers
6) Equal pay and opportunities for women in the Civil Service

If and when one demand was met, it was replaced by another.

---

3. The Six Point Group disbanded in 1981, not because all their demands had been met but because they had too few members. By the 1980s, women were joining different groups and organisations. Imagine you are starting a new Six Point Group. When you have finished this book, work out the six demands your group would campaign for.

Chapter 17   World War Two

Women in an arms factory, 1941.

Although living standards rose during the 1920s and 30s in some parts of Britain, life in the depressed areas remained grim. It only began to improve with the threat of a Second World War. This prompted the government to put money into the old heavy industries and start building tanks, aircraft and ships so that Britain could fight again if necessary. In 1939, the threat became real. Britain and France declared war on Germany. Once again, the war was a mixed blessing for women. For many, it was a time of independence and greater freedom. It was also a time of hard work, long hours, loneliness and grief.

At first, many women lost their jobs as the demand dropped for ordinary goods such as clothes. By 1941 all women had to sign on at a labour exchange. They were given jobs in industry, in the armed forces and as ambulance workers, firefighters, air-raid wardens, aircraft construction workers, farm workers etc.

War work

'War work certainly made many women independent for the first time. Suddenly you could earn your own money and spend it how you wished. We had more freedom.'   (Mrs Crane)

'I went to the Leeds branch (of the bank) as a secretary. . . . Gradually they put us on the jobs that the men were doing, and I ended up on this very busy counter, at the age of 23. In those days no men went on the counter at 23. They had to be at least 30, and before [this they had to be] a cashier, which no girl ever was. My salary remained exactly the same. . . . The bank never paid the ladies any more for doing men's work.'
(Joy Brown)

'For many women the war became liberating. . . . It took them out from under the eyes of their neighbours and all the conventions and social pressures they had been under . . . it was tremendously important for them to find out what they could do . . . not only in doing the work but managing their families and affairs while the men were away. I watched a whole lot of women bloom when they found out they could do all these things they had been told they couldn't do . . . they enjoyed the feeling that they could learn and put their hands to anything that turned up. I watched the older women find that they were necessary. We were all necessary and needed. The country couldn't get on without us.'   (Tess)

The women's Land Army did much farm work.

'Before the war you didn't get a lot of married women working. When the war came ... for the first time I was working with women over twenty. We were happy working. I don't think we ever went back to the fireside in the same way again.'

(Ivy Jones)

'For women it was marvellous that they could get away from home, but probably more so for the upper middle class, where the daughter was stuck at home until she married.... [working class] women said "but we've always gone out to work. We had to, we couldn't have kept our families without." We forget about those women who were doing dreary jobs with terrible pay, but they always knew they had to work, so for them the war wasn't so different, but it gave them the opportunity for better pay.'

(Tess, *What did you do in the War, Mum?*)

---

1. Using these quotes, describe how war work changed women's attitudes to work and to themselves.

Post-war blues

'We got our independence during the war and what we didn't have then, we made sure we got after.'

(Lisa Haddon)

The war ended in 1945. Women workers were in a stronger position than they had been in 1918. They had had some success in gaining equal treatment. The government had set up many nurseries to help working women. In 1943 the trade union movement agreed that women wage earners had equal rights to employment. They also agreed that a person's sex should not determine how much they get paid for a job. The 1944 Education Act made it illegal to sack a teacher when she married.

However, it was not long before women found the freedom, opportunities, jobs and wages they had enjoyed during the war were beginning to slip away.

'Going to live at home again was pretty grim, because Dad was always very strict. It was like having your wings clipped.'

(Joan Welch)

'When all the men came back after the war, the bank said, "Thank you very much for doing all the work for our men while they've been away, but we are not going to have ladies on the counter. Now you've got to teach the men." Instead of having four of us (women) on the counter, they had seven men. We went back to the jolly old machines, the ledger machines and the statement machines, and the shorthand and typing ... we didn't get paid extra for teaching the men.'

(Joy Brown)

'After the war I wanted to get a job, because my husband was on poor pay and I thought – we're not living from hand to mouth. I worked for a company in their records department. One man told me that the way he got his job back was by an elderly man who worked there saying to one woman: "You know you're married and ought not to need a job, and all the time you're staying here the bloke who used to do your job before the war is out of work." That woman only worked another month.... The firm hadn't asked her to leave. The men did.'

(Eileen Smith, *What did you do in the War, Mum?*)

Until 1944 women teachers had to give up their jobs when they married. After this date, they won the right to carry on working.

Girls
Put your bags here

---

2. (a) Why did Eileen want a job? (b) Why did the woman in her story leave her job? (c) What does this tell us about pressures on working women at the time?

---

3. On your own or in groups, do a project on Women, Work and World War Two. Make an illustrated frieze of all the different jobs women did. Collect more information by asking a neighbour or relative to describe her experiences at this time. How similar are they to the ones in this chapter? Combine this material with photographs and information from library books to either (a) make up a folder or (b) design a poster illustrating the theme.

Chapter 18 Post-war Britain

'After the war some women stayed on [at the factory], but the men did get their jobs back. During the war we were needed; afterwards it was different. A lot of women did want to leave though, to be with their husbands.'

(Bessie Miller,
What did you do in the war, Mum?)

After all the uncertainty and upheaval of the war, many people did want a quiet, settled home life. The government encouraged women's role as home-makers. Their jobs were needed for the men returning from war. This is how one Government Report described women's role:

'In the next 30 years, housewives as mothers have vital work to do in ensuring adequate continuance of the British race and of British ideals in the world.'   (*Beveridge Report*, 1942)

---

1.   What does the Beveridge Report expect women to do following 1942? Is this a forward or backward step in terms of views of women in society? What sort of emotions does this statement appeal to? Explain your answers.

In 1946, in spite of everything that had been said earlier, a government commission rejected the idea of equal pay for industrial work, teaching and the civil service. This time women were better organised. Teachers and civil servants campaigned together. They presented a petition to Parliament. Public support for equal pay was much more widespread. The government was also influenced by the fact that after the war there was a 'baby boom'. More teachers were needed. Women who, until 1944, had had to leave teaching work when they married, had to be attracted back. In 1955 the government awarded women teachers and civil servants equal pay.

The Sixties

The difficult post-war 1950s gave way to the 60s – a time of more jobs, more money and more freedom. The invention of the contraceptive pill seemed to remove the problem of unwanted pregnancy. There was a renewed burst of energy, optimism and hard work by women for equal rights and opportunities. From 1968 the movement for Women's *Liberation* became a powerful force. Over the next decade there were a series of changes in the law which were intended to improve the position of women. Women's Liberation was, however, often the butt of jokes and criticism in the media. The suffrage movement had been attacked in the same way. In 1870 *Punch* magazine commented, 'The women who want women's rights mostly want women's charms.'

---

2.   Look at the two cartoons. There is almost 100 years between them, yet they share a similar attitude. How do they depict women fighting for their rights? Do you think this is fair or relevant? Give reasons for your answer.

AN "UGLY RUSH!"   (*Punch* 1870)

'THE UGLY BRIGADE'

Equal for some

The 1955 equal pay award did not benefit the vast majority of working women. In 1963 the *TUC* produced a Charter for Women. It called for:

1) equal pay for work of equal value
2) better promotion and training opportunities
3) more apprenticeship and re-training schemes
4) better health and welfare conditions

Little notice of the Charter was taken.

Then, in 1968, a group of women working at a Ford's factory went on strike for equal pay. They claimed their work was of equal value to a different grade of men's work. They won support from their union and from much of the public. They were successfully upgraded. That year the TUC agreed that *industrial action* should be used to win equal pay for women. A number of MPs introduced an Equal Pay Bill and an Anti-*Discrimination* Bill, which aimed for equality in all areas, not just wages. In 1970 the Equal Pay Act was passed. It said:

> 'Every woman who does the same or broadly similar work as a man for the same employer at the same place of work has a right to the same rate of pay'.

The Act applied to all types and places of work. It did not apply to employment arrangements about retirement, marriage or death. The government gave firms five years to put the Act into practice. Between 1970 and 1975 women's hourly earnings rose from 63% of men's to being 72.1%. They have remained at around that level ever since.

---

3. Illustrate these figures using a bar chart. Explain the rise since 1970.

Women's earnings as a percentage of men's:
1970:63.1%   1975:72.1%   1976:75.1%   1980:73.5%
1983:74.2%   1984:73.5%   1985:74%   1986:74%

---

4. Illustrate these figures using pie charts. Using them and the poster on page 40 to help you, why do you think that, in spite of the Equal Pay Act, women do not yet earn as much as men?

Woman make up 41.4% of the labour force
38% of working women have dependent children:
  27% of them work part-time
44% of all working women work part-time
Only 25% of women with children under 5 work,
  75% of them part-time

Of Britain's 930 000 one-parent families, nearly 90% are headed by women. They have to support their children on wages which are three-quarters or less than those of men's.

Passing a law was clearly not enough to make sure women receive the same wages as men. Changing the law does not automatically change people's minds.

One of the members of the Six Point Group described how she discovered that the Equal Pay Act did not guarantee equal pay.

> 'After the Equal Pay Act, I went through a shoe factory where they were making men's shoes and women's shoes. There were a lot of women pounding shoes – putting heels on actually. And there were a lot of men in another part putting heels on shoes. I said to the manager "I suppose you have equal pay?" And he said "Oh yes, we have equal pay." So I asked him, "Do you mean to say that the women here running this machine and the men over there running the same machine, get the same pay?" He said "Oh no! Heavens no! Those men are putting heels on men's shoes. The women are putting heels on women's shoes. It's not the same work." (Hazel Hunkins Hallinan)

The main way round the law was how an employer interpreted the wording 'the same or broadly similar work as a man'. This meant that women working in jobs rarely done by men were not really covered by the Act, since their work could not be compared. Or employers could transfer women to jobs where there were no male workers to compare themselves with. Or they could give the women's work a different name and grading to anything done by male workers. Other countries in Europe had adopted a different definition: equal pay for 'work of equal value'. This covers women in all sorts of jobs, not just those which are the same or similar to those done by men, since it is possible that two quite different skills might have the same value. In 1982, after several cases had been taken to the European Court, Britain adopted the same wording.

Chapter 19   Discrimination

Equal pay was only part of the battle. Women were still fighting for equal opportunities in training and jobs. Women still had fewer legal rights than men.

In 1975 the Sex Discrimination Act made it illegal to discriminate against women in the UK in jobs, housing, training and the provision of goods and services. Sex discrimination against women means treating them differently because of their sex and for no other reason.

Discrimination can be direct – for example, when someone is refused a job simply because she is a woman. Discrimination can be indirect. For example, an employer might say that a job is only open to people between certain ages, such as 17 to 28. This is the age when many women take time off to have their children. Far fewer women than men could comply with this rule. A company renting something may insist that a woman must have her husband's signature on the form before they will agree to the arrangement. School teachers and the books they use may give the impression that girls are only capable of certain skills. They may not directly say 'girls can't become scientists', for example, but they may not give them the opportunity to explore such possibilities.

Lack of government support for services such as nurseries is also a kind of indirect discrimination. The number of state nurseries has been reduced since the war – in spite of the baby boom. This makes it very difficult for mothers trying to combine work with childcare. Often they are forced to accept less well paid part-time work or very badly paid homework.

Homeworkers and part-timers earn very low wages. The vast majority are women with children. On top of this, most women do an average of 29 hours unpaid housework per week.

THE TEN WORST PAID JOBS IN BRITAIN ARE DONE BY WOMEN

cleaner
receptionist
counterhand
kitchen hand
sewing machinist
barmaid
check out operator
sales and shop assistant
waitress
hairdresser

More than 2 in 5 employees are WOMEN.
Over two-thirds of the low paid are WOMEN.
1 in 4 households is headed by a WOMAN.
1 in 10 families with children is supported solely by a WOMAN.
In 400,000 married couples the only earners are WOMEN.
NOBODY can live on "pin-money".
Women Demand a Fair Day's Pay!

LOW PAY unit

'I went through my school physics book and counted 80 pictures of people doing experiments. Only one of these was a girl, all the rest were male. In the series of French books used from 1st to 5th years, the girls are always shown staying at home helping their mothers with the housework, while the boys are out fishing, and their fathers are at work.' (*Girls Are Powerful*)

'. . . if a girl prefers to opt for needlework and art instead of metalwork and technical drawing, she is not making an informed choice unless someone has explained to her what this may mean in terms of job and pay later on . . . the choice careers still seemed to be working with animals and children, while the boys hog the computers'.

'Mandy became a mother's help. Only gradually she realised that the pay is too low for saving and if you lose your job you lose your place to live. . . . "The careers advice I got wasn't all that good . . .

they didn't teach us about what it was going to be like when we left.... I'd really have loved to do metalwork or something that only boys could do. If you were a girl you were going to be either a secretary or a cook or a nurse – the girls were always pushed into doing typing."'

'... a couple of girls at school went into engineering and the boys treated them with amazement and contempt.' (*Joanne*)

'... closing day nurseries ... means that divorced or deserted mothers will have to live on supplementary benefit rather than being able to earn their own living.'

'One thing I've noticed is that you'll get shops with two part-timers instead of one full-time, and they don't divide it so that each gets half the full wage. It'll be £15 each, say, instead of the £50.'
(Louise, single mother, *Kitchen Sink, Or Swim?*)

---

1. Pick out two of the above quotes and explain how they demonstrate different kinds of discrimination.

Equal Opportunities Commission

The Equal Opportunities Commission was set up to watch over the way the Equal Pay and Sex Discrimination Acts were put into practice. People can bring complaints to the Commission and ask it to investigate a problem. There have been many cases – not all successful.

Sometimes cases show up loopholes in the law. In 1976 Mrs Meeks claimed unlawful sex discrimination because she worked as a part-time secretary and earned a lower amount per hour than the full-timers. She claimed that this amounted to discrimination against women, because almost all part-timers are women. Her claim was rejected because the Sex Discrimination Act does not apply to pay. But a claim under the Equal Pay Act would not succeed either, unless she could compare herself with a man doing the same job – and there were no full-time male secretaries in her office.

---

2. Using the information above and from the end of Chapter 18 explain in what ways you think the original equal pay law needed rewriting.

Many people think that the women's movement died down after winning the vote and that it only came to life again in the 1960s and 70s. But without the work of the Six Point Group, the Women's Co-operative Guild and other organisations the *legislation* of the 1970s would not have come about.

---

3. Look at the Time Chart. Make a list of the legislation passed in the 1970s which improved women's legal position. Then explain in more detail why you think the Matrimonial Proceedings and Property Act was important.

Divorce

A third of marriages in Britain end in divorce. Figures show that very few women with children receive adequate *alimony* and most become very much poorer after divorce. Very few children get places in free state nurseries, so most working mothers have to pay child-minding costs – out of wages which are rarely equal to men's.

---

4. Do you agree with this statement and its conclusion?

'Liberation has brought freedom for men and poverty for women and children ... the only answer is to *ensure* that women can earn as much as men.'

---

5. Over one week, do a survey of family advertisements on TV and in magazines. What effect do you think the kind of image below can have on young people's expectations of their future roles? Do you think they encourage girls to see work as a stop-gap until marriage, after which they will be 'looked after' financially? If so, do you think this matters and why? Think about your answer to question 4 and the information on divorce before you answer this.

Advertisers and the media often present us with this image of the "average" family. The truth is that families made of working dad, non-working mum and two children are only 5.2% of all UK households.

Chapter 20   One World

The booming 1960s and 70s have given way to the more depressed 80s. There are fewer state nurseries, home helps or old people's centres. It is largely women who take on the responsibility of caring for children and the elderly. Unemployment is growing. New technology has made many jobs redundant and opened up others, particularly in computer science.

Some people say Britain will never return to full employment. They believe that we must learn to use our leisure time in ways that are productive and fulfilling. This way we can avoid the feelings of uselessness and failure that unemployment so often causes. Some men experience these feelings when they retire, because they have developed so few interests outside their work. Women, on the other hand, tend to cope with retirement more successfully. As well as working, they have usually had the bulk of family and domestic responsibilities. Women who don't work sometimes suffer from depression in the period when their children are grown up but have not yet produced grandchildren.

---

1.   **Do you agree with this statement? Give reasons for your answer.**

> 'If men and women shared family and work more equally, men might be able to enjoy old age without feeling redundant, and women avoid the depressions of middle age. They would also have a lot more in common.'   (*The Role of Women*)

Interdependence

Workers in Britain are also affected by events outside the country, such as changes in the pattern of world trade. The textile and electronic industries – which employ many women – are declining in Europe and North America. Their place in the world market has been won by workers in the new industrial centres, such as Hong Kong, Taiwan and India. This has meant a clash between the interests of women workers in different countries, although in each case women are being employed because they are cheap labour. Traditionally women have felt a strong bond with each other, wherever they live, because they share so many experiences, such as child birth, child care, providing food and family support, discrimination, *exploitation* of labour. These common bonds – good and bad – mean they are often able to communicate a level of friendship and understanding, whatever their language or culture. Women's groups today form a network of support and friendship throughout the globe. As one British journalist put it:

> 'It's a bit like belonging to an international order of missionary nuns, with all the advantages of kind mothers and sisters with ever-open doors and none of the obvious disadvantages.'
> (Jill Tweedie, *The Guardian*, 28.12.1979)

---

2.   **Explain what you think these lines of poetry mean. Do you agree?**

> '... as a woman I have no country.
> As a woman I want no country. As a
> woman my country is the whole world.'
> (Virginia Woolf)

The same but different

In 1975 women throughout the world took part in events to celebrate International Women's Year. It was also the start of the United Nations Decade for Women. The Decade ended in 1985 with a conference in Nairobi, Kenya. Thousands of women came from all over the world to share their experiences. They discussed the changes, improvements, successes and failures that had taken place over the ten years. They described the new laws, government departments and organisations which had emerged.

The conference confirmed how varied women's experiences, attitudes, circumstances and values were. Many people came away with a greater understanding of these differences, as well as of the shared concerns. For example, women living and working in a religious state, with religious laws and customs to obey, have different problems and strengths to women living in a country such as Britain, where many people feel their lives are barely affected by religion.

Sometimes women from Asia, Africa and South America feel Europeans and North Americans are too quick to tell them what to do, and do not always appreciate that they have different concerns and, more importantly, different ways of tackling them. The conference helped people to understand and respect women's different demands and needs.

The female stars of popular television programmes such as Dallas are always slender, attractive and beautifully dressed. Do you think most women look like them? Do you think such images make women wish they looked like them? If so, do you think this a good thing? Give reasons for your answer.

Many non-western societies value the wisdom and experience a woman gains with age more than her youthful looks.

For example, many westerners condemn arranged marriages as 'barbaric', believing that the only good marriage is a love marriage. Yet it can be argued that this romantic view of marriage is equally *oppressive*. Many western women are desperately concerned with their appearance because youth and beauty are so important to attract 'your man'.

Arranged marriages are built on a different principle: that love will grow out of marriage rather than lead to marriage. *Compatibility* is more important than looks. Marriage is a difficult relationship and neither system has all the answers. An unhappy arranged marriage may be particularly bad, for the woman is often in the less powerful position. At the same time, the ease with which westerners can divorce may sometimes mean that a couple give up too easily on a relationship which just needs more time.

3. Read this extract carefully and explain in your own words what Buchi Emecheta is saying about the status of older women (and men) in African and in American society. Do you agree?

'A 50 year old American woman with grey hair is old; a 50 year old American male with grey hair is dignified: a 50 year old Ibo (Nigerian) woman with grey hair is in her prime and almost as dignified as a man.... Western civilisation has prepared [the woman] only for her youth, and has told her she can appeal to men only as a young woman.... So the African woman claims to be older than she is, and the American woman is forever claiming to be young.' (B. Emecheta, *Women: A World Report*)

4. Think carefully about the advantages and disadvantages of 'arranged' and 'love' marriages. Make two lists and compare them with your friends' answers. Discuss whether the advantages of the two systems are the same for men as they are for women.

Chapter 21   Acts or Attitudes?

'The battle for women's rights has been largely won.'   (Prime Minister Margaret Thatcher)

Around the same time this was claimed, a Member of Parliament said:

'If the Good Lord had intended us all having equal rights to go out to work, he wouldn't have created men and women.'   (Patrick Jenkin, MP, 1979)

Clearly, people's ideas and attitudes lag behind the laws which make equal opportunities possible. There are still battles to be fought. The figures below and the quotes from today's teenagers reveal that equality is more than a question of legal rights.

Women are still very much in the minority in the engineering, computing and scientific professions.

Education

Examination passes (1984)

Girls 53.6%	CSE Grade 1
Girls 51.2%	GCE O Level
Girls 47%	GCE A Level

Girls took mainly arts subjects and languages and were out numbered by boys in maths, science and computer studies.

Girls 46%to university	Pupils with 2 or more A Levels
Boys 58%to university	
Girls 41.5%	Graduates
Girls 31.8%	Postgraduates

Girls tend to study less practical subjects, while boys choose courses more directly related to jobs and career-building.

'Getting a boyfriend is bound up with impressing other people. You get status when you're going out with a boy.'

'Boys tend to think we're all weaklings – but engineering and other work they think is just for men doesn't even need the strength that nursing needs.'
   (*Girls Are Powerful*)

1. **In groups, discuss:**
   (a) Are women's brains really more suited to arts than science subjects?
   (b) Is it somehow more 'feminine' to study English Literature than electronics?
   (c) Are girls reluctant to compete with boys or to be seen as brainy?
   (d) Do girls tend to see success as having a boyfriend, not good exam results or a good job?

Employment

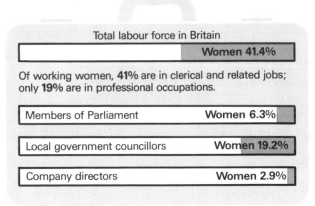

Total labour force in Britain	
	Women 41.4%

Of working women, **41%** are in clerical and related jobs; only **19%** are in professional occupations.

Members of Parliament	Women 6.3%
Local government councillors	Women 19.2%
Company directors	Women 2.9%

2. **In groups, discuss:**
   (a) There are few women managers and directors. Does this mean women are less suited to positions of authority?
   (b) Do women have to be better than men to get to the top?
   (c) Are they held back by having children at the time when the career race is fiercest?
   (d) Why are there so few women directors and MPs?
   (e) Should there be a Minister for Women?

In 1987, Deacon Sylvia Mutch became the first woman to conduct a Church of England marriage ceremony in Britain. The same year the Church voted to start the legislation which may eventually allow women to become priests.

---

3. Do a survey among a group of girls and boys of your own age to find out their work ambitions and expectations. Compare the results, using graphics, and write up any conclusions you draw from your survey.

Creative powers

Before the educational reforms of the nineteenth century, many a man – and woman – confused lack of education with lack of intelligence. They stated that women's minds were inferior to men's. Today, such remarks are rare, although not unheard of. However, people still point to lack of achievement in certain spheres as evidence of lack of talent or ability. Some people believe that women are less creative than men. Their 'proof' of this is the fact that there have been so few famous women artists, composers or scientists. But is this because women are less creative or because they have had much less opportunity to develop their creativity?

Men have always been encouraged to be single-minded in their work. Throughout history, the 'difficult' genius is admired and almost always finds a woman, or several, to look after him. Women who are single-minded about their career or talent more often just feel selfish. They are far less likely to find a man prepared to support them in their work and take on their domestic responsibilities. For a woman to be truly single-minded about work can mean sacrificing having a family. Men rarely have to make such a choice.

Remember, too, that in the past, women were taught music and art as attractive accomplishments. Their piano playing, painting and sketching were 'drawing room' skills, designed to please other people, not to fulfil their own creative energies. Children were meant to do that. 'Feminine' arts such as embroidery were not given the status of 'real' art. Until the 1860s women were excluded from colleges of music and art and so from being professional musicians and artists. And it is very difficult to compose for an orchestra when you can't even play in one.

Women writers

One area where women have gained recognition is as writers. In the nineteenth century, novel writing was a reasonably acceptable occupation for women. Journalism was not. Even so, novelists such as Mary Anne Evans (George Eliot) had to use a male name, not only in order to get a publisher to consider her but also to avoid being criticised for writing about 'unladylike' subjects.

The work of many female novelists of that time concentrates on personal matters: family life and relationships. They wrote about what they knew, for often they were excluded from decisions and discussions about politics and current affairs.

Women have been criticised for working on this 'small scale' by those who fail to see its value and richness. Yet this very concern with domestic detail also tells us how hard it has always been for women to break away from household duties and find the time and energy to develop creative talents and interests.

Women's writing – fiction and non-fiction – has become tremendously popular since the 1970s. Many older, forgotten works have been reprinted. They reveal the rich and varied experiences of women in the past, which were often left out of conventional history books.

Chapter 22   The Way Ahead?

Many people in the Women's Movement today are concentrating more on changing attitudes than on changing or making laws. The feminists of centuries ago recognised the vital role of education in changing attitudes. It remains a central issue. But education is more than what we learn in school. It is the messages we receive about our roles from our family, from friends and from society generally.

Girls and boys start reading different material and receiving different messages from an early age. Boys' comics are action-packed and full of heroes having daring escapades in exotic places. Girls' comics are more about romance, clothes and looks, pop stars, and film stars. Girls are encouraged in their romantic fantasies while boys are not encouraged to admit to feelings of love, dependence, uncertainty or weakness. They don't want to be called 'sissy'.

1.   The boys and girls referred to here are all less than 15 years old. What do the quotes tell us about their expectations?

> 'I think the mums tend to favour the boys really . . . my younger brother washes up about once a month, and my mum will go, "Oh its really good of you." I do it all the time.'   (*Girls are Powerful*)

> 'When I have kids, I think I'd be stricter with the girls. . . . I wouldn't make the boys do a lot of things, like clean or dust or anything. . . . They should help a bit, but they shouldn't do the women's work.'   (Debbie, aged 13,)

> 'I have one brother and I play cricket with him and football, but he doesn't play dolls with me. He plays doctors and nurses, and he's the doctor.'   (Diane, age 7, *Fenwomen*)

These attitudes and expectations have their disadvantages for men too. Some feel trapped inside a macho image which doesn't allow them to admit their real emotions, doubts or weaknesses. Some envy women the chance of stopping work for a while and concentrating on their children. Many men would like to be able to spend more time with their families, just as many women would like to spend less time at home.

Most of the action to improve women's status has tried to give them equal opportunities in a man's world. Some people feel we should now be

Many now see an important step towards improving women's status is for men to take on more so-called women's work, to gain pride and enjoyment from it and thus admit its value and importance.

working towards giving men an equal chance in a woman's world. By doing this, we would be acknowledging the positive value of what is regarded, often scornfully, as 'women's work' and 'female emotions'. Women's status really would be raised, once so-called 'female qualities' were so respected that men not only felt comfortable admitting when they shared them – but wanted to develop them when they did not.

> 'The next phase of women's liberation is not to have to prove how tough and *unassailable* you are, but to be unafraid of showing your needs and your *vulnerability* – not because this is slavishly "feminine" in the helpless sense, but because it is what makes us all human.'   (Mary Kenny, 1978)

2.   In groups, discuss whether you agree with this statement.

Time chart

(Laws marked * are described in more detail in the text)

1694   Mary Astell's *A Serious Proposal to the Ladies* published

1792   Mary Wollstonecraft's *Vindication of the Rights of Women* published

1839   Infant's Custody Act*: until this act, the law said a child had only one parent, the father

1848   Queen's College for Women opened

1850   First Girls' Public Day School founded (offering grammar-school education for girls)

1857   Matrimonial Causes Act*

1863   Girls allowed to take Cambridge Examination (equivalent to A level)

1865   Elizabeth Garrett Anderson becomes first woman in Britain to qualify as a doctor

1869   Women in Wyoming, USA, are first to get the vote

1870   Married Women's Property Act*
Education Act: all local authorities to provide schools
Women allowed to be members of School Boards

1873   Three girls pass Cambridge degree but are refused diplomas

1874   Women's Trade Union League founded

1875   Law passed allowing universities to grant women degrees
First women attend Trades Union Congress

1882   Married Women's Property Act*

1886   Guardianship of Infants Act*
Married Women (Maintenance) Act*

1888   Match makers' strike
Women allowed to vote in local elections

1893   First woman factory inspector appointed
Women in New Zealand get the vote

1895   Royal College of Surgeons allow women members

1897   National Union of Women's Suffrage founded in Britain

1902   Women in Australia get the vote

1906   Women in Finland get the vote

1907   Qualifications of Women Act: women can become local councillors
Women in Norway get the vote

1917   Russian Revolution gives vote to women of Russia

1918   Virtually all men over 21 and women over 30 get the vote in Britain
Women over 21 can become MPs

1919   Nancy Astor becomes first woman MP to take her seat in Parliament
Sex Disqualification (Removal) Act: women can become magistrates, jurors, barristers and solicitors
Women admitted as full members of Oxford University

1921   Marie Stopes opens first birth control clinic

1923   Matrimonial Causes Act; women can now divorce for same reasons as men

1925   Guardianship of Infants Act; men and women have equal rights over children; custody of children of divorced parents is to be decided by courts

1928   Women in Britain given vote on equal terms with men

1929   Margaret Bondfield becomes first woman Cabinet Minister

1944   It becomes illegal to dismiss married women teachers

1948   Women admitted as full members of Cambridge University

1955   Women teachers and civil servants win equal pay

1958   Women allowed into House of Lords as life peeresses

1963   The first Women's Charter adopted by the TUC

1970   Equal Pay Act*
Matrimonial Proceedings and Property Act; a women's non-financial contribution to a

household to be taken into account in any split of property after divorce, protecting them from being left with nothing because their contribution to looking after the family has been unpaid

1975 Sex Discrimination Act*
Employment Protection Act: covered maternity leave and pay

1975 Equal Opportunity Commission set up

1976 Domestic Violence Act; gave greater legal protection to women suffering from violence in the home

1979 Margaret Thatcher becomes Britain's first woman Prime Minister

1987 Church of England agrees to consider the ordination of women as priests

Glossary

Words in text

accelerate   speed up
administer   carry out or enforce
alimony   an allowance for living expenses
ambition   what someone wants to achieve, a wish
Board   committee
Board School   government school
campaign   action to arouse public opinion for or against an issue
classical   learned in Latin or Greek
clerical   office
compatibility   ability to get on well together
constitution   a person's body and mind
consumer   one who buys things, a shopper
diplomacy   the art of making arrangements between nations
discrimination   to make a difference between things
economy   matters to do with money
emancipation   freedom from slavery
expectations   what you expected or look forward to achieving
exploitation   make unfair use of
guardian   one who takes care of another
hypocritical   pretending to be something one is not
incapacitated   out of action
illiterate/literate   unable/able to read and write
industrial action   strikes, working to rule
ironic   hiding the real meaning
legislation   process of making laws
liberation   freedom
listless   feeble
lobby   to try to influence
maternity/paternity leave   paid time off work for mothers/fathers when they have a baby
militant   fighting
oppressive   treating people unjustly
patriarchal   under the rule of men
picket   small groups of people who try to persuade others of their cause
promotion   advancement to a better job
rational   logical

shorthand   a system of fast writing using symbols
socialist   one who believes the country's land and wealth belong to everyone
status   a person's state, condition or standing
suffrage   power to vote
suffragettes   women who fought for the right to vote
TUC   Trades Union Council

Words in quotations

abroad   outside the home
bondage   slavery
define   to say what something/one is
embellish   to add grace or beauty to
engine   method
ensure   make certain
entertain   consider
facilitate   to make easier
fetters   chains
impunity   safety from punishment
insipid   without any spirit or energy
inverse   opposite
libel   to make a statement damaging someone's character
minister   to look after
pamper   to please
perpetuate   to make last, to continue
philosophical   lover of wisdom
prating   talking foolishly
prime mover   the one in charge
prohibition   ban
ratio   proportion
scullion   kitchen servant
statutory   made by law
subtleties   fine details
unassailable   cannot be attacked
vagrant   idle, wandering
vulnerability   ability to be hurt
wit   intelligence